BARGELLO

RANDOM HOUSE NEW YORK

note:

Peri-Lusta yarns are obtainable from retailers and stores, under the Peri-Lusta label, but in case of difficulty, write to Paragon Art & Linen Co., Inc., 367 Southern Boulevard, Bronx, New York, for names of your nearest supplier. However, any 3-ply Persian-type yarn can be substituted.

Credits
Cover photograph by Steve Bicknell.
Waistcoat and cushions designed by Martyn Thomas. Dress by Jean Muir.
Other photographs by Chris Lewis, pages 28,39,47, 50; Jim Williams, pages 49,54,55; Camera Press/ IMS/Kjell Nilsson, pages 32,40,41,43; Peter Pugh-Cook, page 36 right; John Carter, page 53; Graham Murrell, page 52 (coat designed by Wendy Bellamy); Graham Henderson, pages 14,15,44,64; Malcolm Aird, page 30; Courtesy of Parham Park, Pull-borough, Sussex, page 1; Museum of the City of New York, page 2, top; Metropolitan Museum of Art, New York, a gift from Mrs. J. Insley Blair, pages 2,3. Welcome Pernelle, page 35.
Stitchery designer: Martyn Thomas.
Consultant: Margaret Beautement.
Art Editor: Amelia Edwards.
Co-ordinator: Susan Pinkus.
Fashion designs by Wendy Bellamy.
Graphs and art work by Alan Rhodes.

Manufactured in Great Britain
First American Edition

contents

Florentine Flashback   1
Introducing Bargello   4
Zigzag   4
Flame   4
Geometric trellis   6
Curvature   6
Brocade   9
Basic Stitching   10
Patterns Galore
Gothic   16
Romanesque   16
Pomegranate   16
Stars and Stripes   18
3-D Boxes   18
Honeycomb   20
Trellis Major   20
Aurora Borealis   22
Fountain Brocade   22
Diamonds within Diamonds   25
Chevron Trellis   25
Prickly Pine   27
Carnation   27
Florentine Designs
Little gifts
Hairband   31
Clasp belt   31
Lighter case   31
Glasses case   31
Compact case   31
Florentine flap-over bag   32
Bargello pillows   34
Strip designs
Belts   36
Caftan trim   37
Quick-to-finish wallhanging   38
Set and match   40
Brighten up a chair   42
Color at your feet
Fender stool   45
Wastepaper basket   45
Footstool   45
Colorful comfort—slippers   46
Shoulder stroller   48
Speedy stitchery   50
Sampler bags   50
Coats of many colors   52
Shaping up with Florentine   55
Fashion ideas   56
Finishing instructions   60

The magnificent bed-hangings at Parham Park, Sussex, England, are among the most beautiful examples of bargello or Florentine

florentine flashback

stitchery. Turn for some intriguing insight into the origin and revival of this remarkable stitch craze.

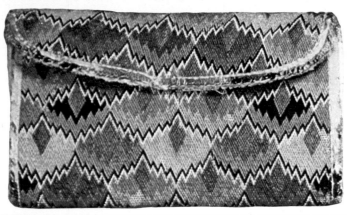

A fascinating history

Suddenly in vogue again, Florentine work has actually been a very popular form of embroidery for many hundreds of years. A few early examples even date back as far as the late 13th century, by which time embroiderers had already found it to be one of the quickest and most economical ways of covering a large area of material. It was not until the late 16th and 17th centuries, however, that this sort of canvas embroidery was experimented with more widely throughout Europe. Soon, variations on the basic Florentine stitch were also developed – Hungarian Point and Flame among them. Although its true origin is shrouded in mystery, many believe that Florentine stitch, despite its name, was first worked not in Italy, but in Hungary. One attempt to explain its history runs as follows. It seems a

Hungarian princess married into the Italian Medici family, bringing with her a magnificently embroidered trousseau. Supposedly, she then set about teaching the ladies of the Florentine Court this art of Punto Ungero or "Hungarian Point". Further legend, however, tells that it was actually Elizabeth of Hungary who thought up this ingeniously economical use of stitches, to be worked by peasants during times when wool was short. Florentine work has also been widely known for many years as "Bargello". Yet another traditional tale explains how it came to get this name: but this time, the account is probably more factual. The Hungarian Princess, Jadwiga, is known to have left her home at the age of 13 and to have married King Vladislav of Poland in 1383. Once wed, she set about displaying her talents as an embroideress. Among the items she worked is

a bishop's cope in Florentine stitch, which incorporates the arms of both Poland and Hungary. Part of it still exists today. Now, King Vladislav's family name was Jagiello; and it seems very probable that, over a period, this name may well have become corrupted by foreign tongues, to be known by the pronunciation "Bargello". The needlework done by Queen Jadwiga may therefore also have taken this name.

Whatever the truth, ironically enough there is no connection at all between the Jagiello line and the noble Podesta family who built the famous 13th century Palace of Bargello in Florence. Yet, by complete coincidence, this building – which became part of the National Museum in 1857 – houses an elegant set of 17th century chairs, covered in traditional Bargello work. (A modified version of the design can be found on page 8).

Above and left, American wallets dating from before 1900. They remain only slightly faded and are worked in exciting Florentine patterns featuring carnations and flickering flames.

Right Florentine— covered chair from the Metropolitan Museum of Art, New York.

These chairs cannot be linked directly to the Bargello Palace simply because they were not purchased by the museum authorities until 23rd September 1886 from a Signor Menichetti! Still, legend persists; and the fact that the Bargello Palace was once a political prison has led to another somewhat fanciful thought. It is held by some that prisoners awaiting trial used to do embroidery in the palace cells. Here they are said both to have invented and mastered the art of the so-called Bargello stitch. Inspection of these cells – miniscule, below ground level and without natural light of any kind – leaves one in no doubt as to the improbability of this myth.

Most of the surviving Florentine of the pre-18th century period is in the form of bed curtains or wall hangings. In England the treasure-house of this type of embroidery is,

of course, Parham Park in Sussex. The collection here must be one of the finest. The crowning glory of the house is undoubtedly the magnificent four-poster bed in the Great Chamber, surrounded by four curtains, three top valances and three mattress valances, all in Florentine. These most beautiful hangings, shown on page 1, were worked during the reign of Charles II, and are embroidered on strips of canvas only 9½ inches wide, in silk and wool. Each strip is joined by a narrow worked border of the same stitch, disguising the seams. The effect is regal, without being overbearing.

Early American examples

Popular with embroiderers all over Europe, including England, it was inevitable that the technique of Florentine should have been carried across the Atlantic to the American

colonies. The beautiful examples shown – all from American collections – are dated from before 1800, yet the colors of the yarns are only slightly faded. The wallets, which are dated between 1750 and 1800, feature carnation and flickering flame patterns.

The brilliantly colored purse which is worked with the name of the owner, Hendrick Rutgers, is also worked with the date of its execution – 1761. The Queen Anne type wing chair, dated 1725 and now in the Metropolitan Museum of Art, New York, is a curiosity. The front of the chair, as seen, is worked in Florentine stitch. The back of the chair is rather surprisingly adorned with a magnificent panel, freely worked in crewel wools, showing various aspects of hunting – running deer, pursuing hounds, birds in flight, ducks on a pond, all against an undulating landscape.

3

introducing bargello...

Most straightforward forms of Bargello stitch are worked over four or six threads of canvas at once, covering impressively large areas in no time at all. Naturally, this provides added stimulus for the beginner, anxious to see results as soon as possible.

Zigzag and Flame

These are perhaps the very simplest and most characteristic patterns. Each row of a separate color is worked horizontally across the canvas, with either a step up or a step down from stitch to stitch. There is no breaking off to change the color of the thread. Once a line of one color has been worked across the canvas as a basis on which to work, all others follow suit.

Flame stitches, on the other hand, best achieve their success by means of subtle shading of the colors from row to row, each slightly different from its neighbor.

Zigzag

The zigzag is the simplest pattern of all. It is worked from a base line and repeats every ten stitches. The yarn is taken over four threads and back two. Work an exciting color experiment to give you confidence in the stitch and working methods.

In Peri-Lusta yarn: one horizontal repeat = S. 10 / W. ¾″ / H. 1″ / Y. 9″.
For key to abbreviations, see page 10.

With D.M.C. Tapestry: width, height and yardage will be marginally less than with Peri-Lusta yarn over one repeat, due to difference in canvas size. (See chart on page 11).

Flame

Flame stitch is worked over four threads and back one. It is important to start in the center of the canvas with the apex of the highest peak. The colors progress from white through the palest apricot to the darkest burnt orange, and then from the darkest of golden browns to gold. The progression from white is then repeated.

Peri-Lusta colors: 1. 455 white; **2.** 138 pale orange; **3.** 804 dark orange; **4.** 803 dark orange; **5.** 802 dark orange; **6.** 136 dark orange; **7.** 135 dark orange; **8.** 451 brown; **9.** 205 dark gold; **10.** 207 gold; **11.** 445 pale gold.
One horizontal repeat = S. 36 / W. 2½″ / H. 2″ / Y. 27″.
For key to abbreviations, see page 10.

With D.M.C. Tapestry: 11 colors to your choice. Width, height and yardage will be marginally smaller than with Peri-Lusta yarn over one repeat, due to difference in canvas size. (See chart on page 11).

4

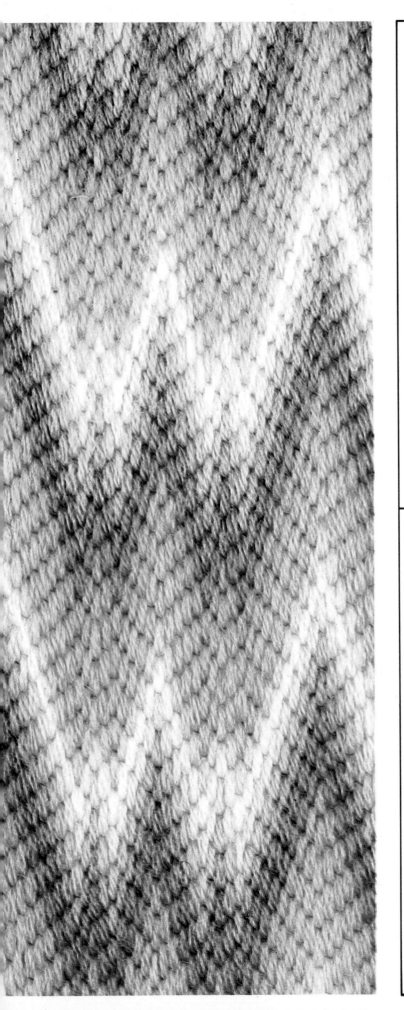

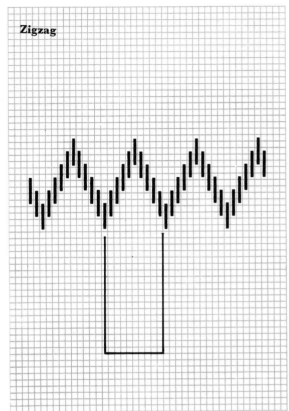

Zigzag

Exciting effects are achieved with use of vivid, contrasting colors.

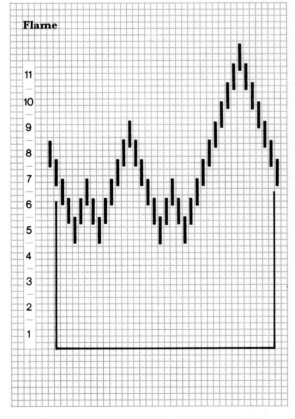

Flame

11
10
9
8
7
6
5
4
3
2
1

Flame patterns lend themselves well to subtle color shading.

Geometric Patterns

Zigzag and flame designs can easily be developed into the slightly more complex designs of Trellises, Diamonds, Squares and Basket Weaves. Here, pattern base lines are worked diagonally across the canvas instead of horizontally. But the same general principal of stitch remains.

Geometric trellis

This pattern is worked over four canvas threads and back two. Work from the top center of the canvas and stitch the first continuous line of the brown and white trellis down to the bottom of the left-hand side. Block in a half-diamond in orange, and continue across the canvas to position the first trellis row correctly. After this, block in the three orange tones one by one. This method saves constant rethreading of the needle with different colors, and applies to all the trellis designs.

Peri-Lusta colors: 1. 120 brown; **2.** 455 white; **3.** 139 light orange; **4.** 136 dark orange; **5.** 138 medium orange.

One repeat = S. 31 (outline): 16 (color **4.**): 24 (color **3.**): 22 (color **5.**) / W. 1½″ / H. 3″ / Y. 27″ (outline): 11″ (color **4.**): 18″ (color **3.**) 17″ (color **5.**).

For key to abbreviations, see page 10.

With D.M.C. Tapestry: 5 colors to your choice. Width, height and yardage will be marginally smaller than with Peri-Lusta yarn over one repeat, due to difference in canvas size. (See chart on page 11).

Curvature Patterns

Zigzag, flame and geometric patterns are achieved with straight lines. It is also possible, however, to achieve an illusion of regular curves. This is done by placing individual stitches next to one another without a step up or step down, and varying the number of stitches in progression. Thus the flame patterns can be transformed into rolling waves and garlands; and the diamond and trellis designs into ogees, hearts and circles.

Once this has been mastered, it will be possible to form almost any pattern at all. Using a variety of colors, you can even produce the very intricate Carnation on page 26. Although a simplified version of an original 17th century design, it is still quite a complex pattern to achieve.

Curvature

This design is worked over four threads of the canvas and back two. Work a line of black horizontally across the canvas and then a line of white on either side of it. These are the only continuous horizontal lines. The pattern is divided into vertical bands. There is a progression of six shades, in addition to the black and white. Adjacent bands progress in opposite ways – one from the palest to the darkest, and its neighbor from the darkest to the palest. The color change begins at the low center point and the stitch after the high center point.

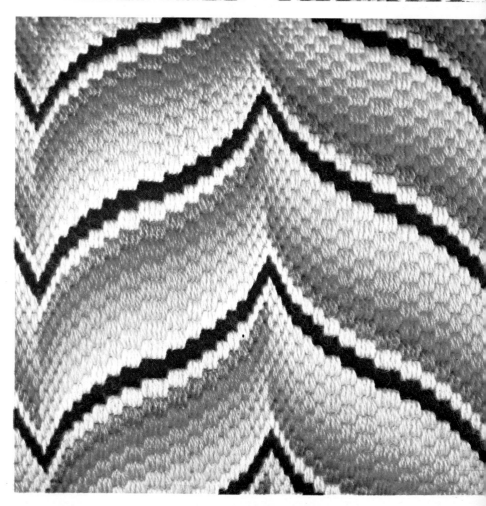

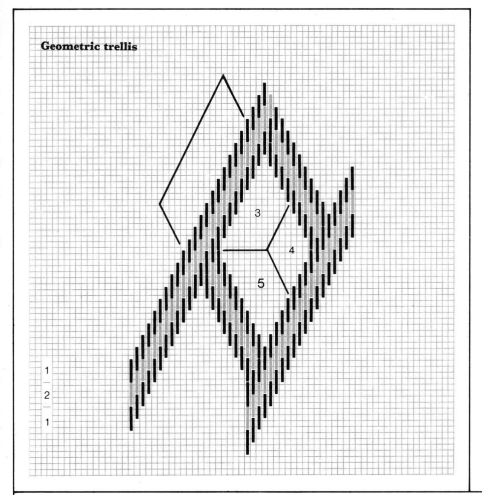

Geometric trellis

Left A geometric trellis design taking you one step beyond the basic zigzag. Trellis lines are worked first. Colored diamonds complete the pattern.

Below A curvature design in which only the rows of black and white are worked right across the canvas. Other rows change color tone at center points.

Curvature continued
Peri-Lusta colors: 1. 455 white; **2.** 285 black; **3.** 411 khaki; **4.** 135 dark orange; **5.** 136 orange; **6.** 137 orange; **7.** 138 orange; **8.** 139 pale orange.
One repeat = S. 91 (color **1.**): 46 and 44 (alternate bands to right and left of center) / W. 7″ / H. 3½″ /. 3½ yds. (color **1.**): 1½ yds. and 1 yd. (alternate bands).
For key to abbreviations, see page 10.

With D.M.C. Tapestry: 8 colors to your choice. Width, height and yardage will be marginally smaller than with Peri-Lusta yarn over one repeat, due to difference in canvas size. (See chart on page 11).

Curvature

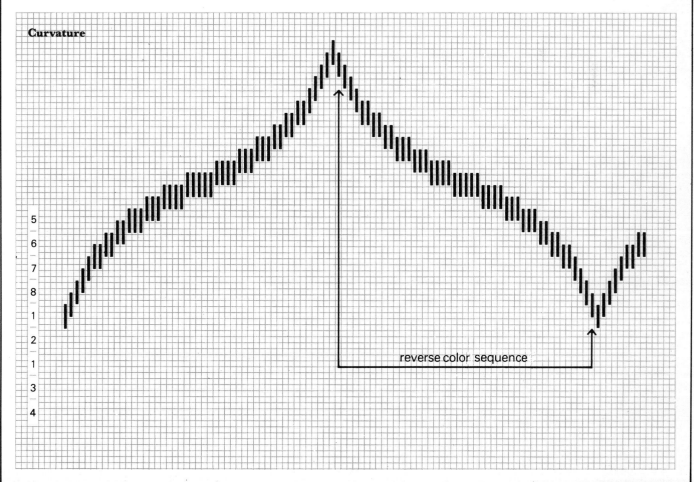

reverse color sequence

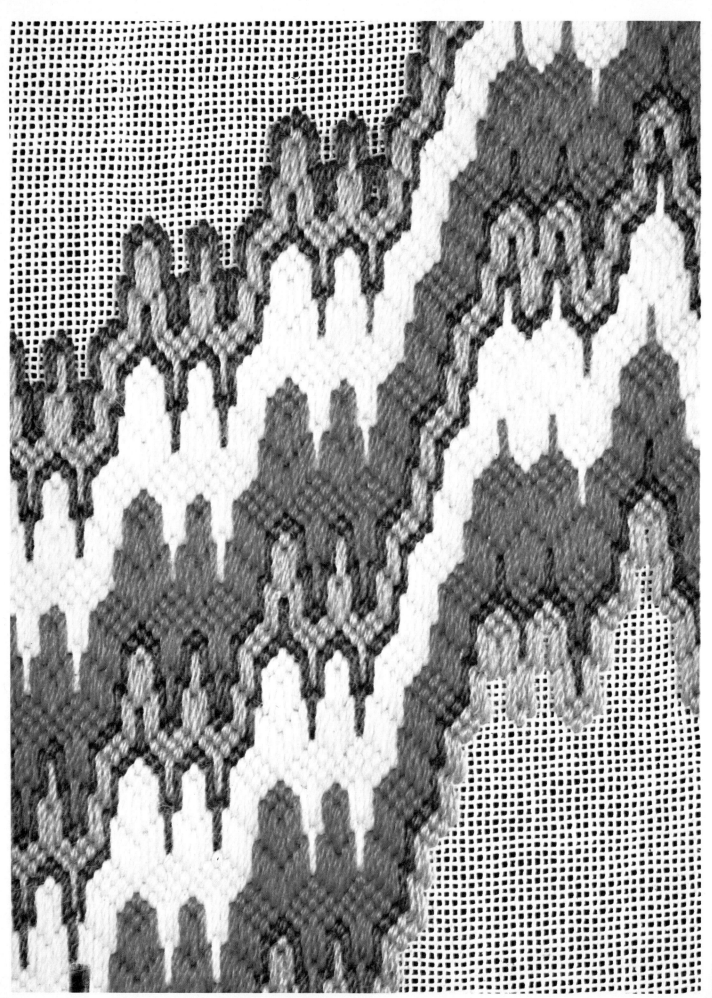

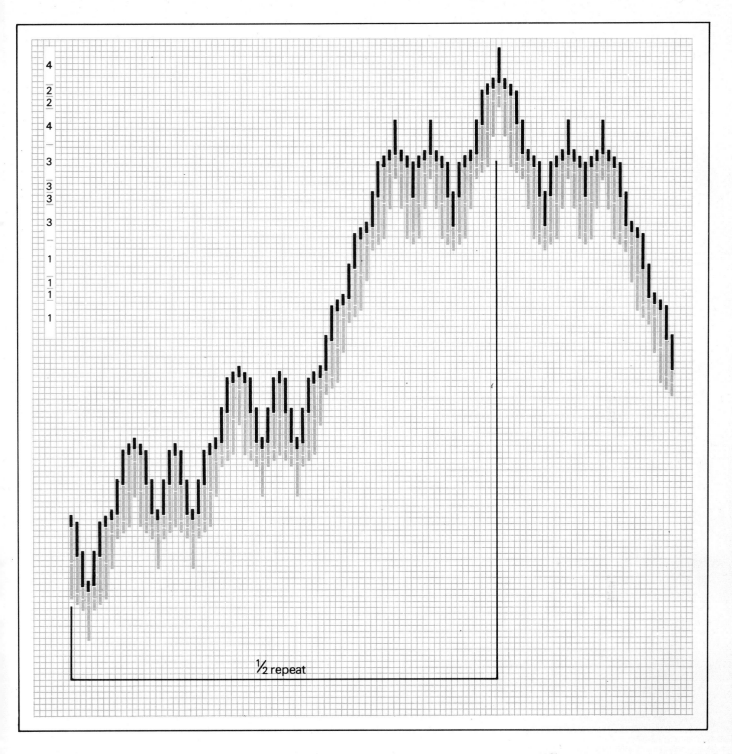

½ repeat

Brocaded Designs

Most applications of Florentine stitch produce a surface which is smooth and regular. It is, however, also possible to get a combination of both pattern and texture. By alternating the length of horizontally adjacent stitches as well as those immediately above or below each other, a pleasant sculptured effect results. This is, of course, more painstaking and requires greater concentration. But the resulting embossed quality makes it stronger and more durable, and the embroidery is therefore suitable for upholstery use. However, final wearing quality will depend a good deal on the quantity of yarn at the back of the work. A small, thin stitch, for instance, tends to wear

quickly with the friction between the reverse of the canvas and a padded stool top. The effective brocade design shown is derived from the Bargello chair covers, now housed at the National Museum in Florence and referred to on page 2.

Brocade design

This design is worked over six canvas threads, back one; and over two, back one. The stitch order repeats every three rows. A half repeat is shown which mirrors or reverses. It is interesting to note that the stitches immediately above or below each other go in pairs: that is, two of the smaller stitches go with two of the longer ones, regardless of colors. This is an excellent check if in doubt.

A sculptured, embossed design making embroidery particularly suitable for upholstery use.

Peri-Lusta shades: 1. 257 dark pink; **2.** 258 pale pink; **3.** 455 white; **4.** 722 peacock. One repeat = S. 141 / W. 10″ / H. 6¾″ / Y. 3 yds.

For key to abbreviations, see page 10.

With D.M.C. Tapestry: 4 colors to your choice. Width, height and yardage will be marginally smaller than with Peri-Lusta yarn over one repeat, due to difference in canvas size. (See chart on page 11).

basic stitching

Color choosing

Florentine embroidery lends itself to adventurous use of color. The softening effect of a range of tones from dark to light in one color is strengthened by a sharp contrast in another. But because the style of the embroidery is bold, it can also take on correspondingly vivid shades. The vitality of many pieces, both historic and modern, depends on a range of colors from very dark to light, as well as a variety of tones. A color card is not expensive to buy and very worthwhile for the inspirations it can evoke. The yarns are in most cases fastened to the cards in straight rows, as they will appear when stitched as a Satin Stitch. From sheets of paper, cut out an oblong shape to fit the color range. The colors of your choice will stand out clearly, and it is easy to see whether they are sufficiently rich and varied.

Key to charts

Pages 4 – 9 show basic patterns for the many exciting designs to be found in the Pattern Library on pages 14 – 27.
Before you begin stitching, a glance at the yarn chart which follows will give you yarn and canvas sizes used throughout the book, and details of alternatives.
Base pattern and pattern library charts are all drawn to the same system.
For the horizontal patterns, a base line is given and one single repeat is marked. Where necessary, a numbered key shows the color sequence used in the pattern given. The listed colors on the instructions are numbered to correspond.
The base line is the shape of the pattern. The color sequence forms its rhythm or character.
The trellis patterns and reversed horizontal line patterns are shown as outlines with the sequence of color numbers as a cross section through the center line.
Where necessary, the color sequence within the outline is shown as a separate diagram. A bracket will indicate the extent of one repeat.

Abbreviation notes

Abbreviations at the end of the base pattern and pattern library notes are as follows:
One repeat = S. (stitches)
W. (width)
H. (height over one color row of the repeat)
Y. (yardage)

Canvas

Florentine embroidery is best worked on single thread canvas. The stitches lie side by side and cover the canvas closely. The size of the canvas is denoted by the number of woven threads to the inch. See chart on page 11 for comparative sizes.

Yarns

Most of the patterns shown here are worked with yarns manufactured for embroidery. Yarn makes, color numbers and quantities are given for the finished embroidery. See page 11 for a chart giving yardage of all yarns quoted in the book. You can, of course, use any yarn you choose on an appropriate canvas, but the quantities and scale of the design will vary accordingly. Experimenting outside the given range of thread can make for exciting highlights. Many unusual knitting and crochet yarns are available, including cotton and acrylic. Choose any which will cover the canvas adequately. If the thread is too thick for the size of the canvas, it will be difficult to stitch, and the finished result will be lumpy rather than smooth in texture. If the thread is too thin, then the final effect lacks vitality. Canvas showing between the stitches spoils the crisp effect of the patterns. The stitching is flat and therefore shows any yarn to advantage, catching the light with full depth of color.
This effect will change slightly with each type of yarn, depending largely on whether it is tightly or loosely spun. Tapestry yarn loosely spun, catches the light more than crewel wool which is more highly spun. Use the latter in several strands to cover a 16 or 18 threads to the inch canvas. Personal experiment will show how much is needed. About three strands of crewel wool on an 18 threads to the inch canvas is a guide line. But this will vary with the make of yarn and the tension of your stitching. It is perfectly possible to take apart yarns of several ply to form, say, 1 or 2 ply; or to add further strands to the yarn as it occurs in the ball or skein.

Estimating yarn quantities

With practice, estimating yarn quantities required for a particular design becomes more and more a matter of routine. But at first you may prefer to buy extra yarn as and when you require it. The following methods of calculation are useful for fairly advanced stitchery. Initially, they may appear complicated. But many find the mathematics of Florentine a fascination in itself, and the whole yarn assessment procedure soon becomes clear.

Estimating for small areas

Start by cutting an 18 inch length. Stitch as much of the pattern repeat as this will work. (If the canvas is not well covered, adjust the number of strands in the needle). Count the number of part patterns (i.e. the part of the pattern you are able to work with 18 inches) needed to work one complete row. Multiply by the 18 inch length. Multiply again by the number of rows in each separate color. It is

then easy to calculate from the yardage given on the manufacturer's label whether one or more skeins or balls are required of each color.

Calculation example. If you require $3\frac{1}{2}$ lengths of 18 inches to work one row, this totals 63 inches. If you then require 12 lines of this particular color for the pattern, you will therefore need 63 x 12 inches of yarn, amounting to 756 inches. If the skeins you are using contain, say, 10 yards of yarn, this is the equivalent of 10 x 36 inches (360). Divide the number of inches of yarn required (i.e. 756) by the number of inches in the skein to find out how many skeins are needed. 756 divided by 360 comes to just over 2. It would therefore be necessary to buy 3 skeins of yarn in this particular color.
For patterns other than those worked from a base line, work a length in each motif on a spare piece of canvas and work out the number of sections of each motif in the same way as for the parts of one row.

Estimating for larger areas

Requirements for the basic patterns and the Pattern Library are given in Peri-Lusta 3-ply Persian yarn (on 14 threads to the inch canvas) and **D.M.C. Tapestry** wool (on 16 threads to the inch canvas). With each pattern are given the number of stitches in one repeat, the width and height of the resulting repeat and the working yardage.
From this formula it is comparatively easy to work out the appropriate amount of yarn needed to cover large canvas areas.

Calculation example. To work a 16″ x 12″ pillow in Flame Stitch (see base pattern on page 5) you will need to add, as in all canvas measurements, an extra 4 inches to the finished size to allow for blocking and making. (i.e. You will require a piece of canvas 20″ x 16″.)
To assess quantities of Peri-Lusta 3-ply Persian yarn, consider the following. For this same Flame stitch pattern, the repeat is $2\frac{1}{4}″$ wide, height 2″ and yarn length 27″. Across the 16 inch width, there will be just over six repeats of the pattern. You will need about 5 yards of the yarn for each row. There are 11 color rows, each stitch taken over 4 threads. From the dark base to the light highpoint is about 3 inches. The sequence of colors will therefore repeat about four times over the 12 inch depth. Multiply the 5 yards for each row by the 4 rows of each color. 24 yards. (Remember to add extra yardage to fill in the part patterns at the top and bottom.) 8.8 yards are contained in each skein of this particular yarn. It would therefore be advisable to buy four skeins in each color. With any yarn over, make a cord to trim the pillow, or try some of the fascinating experiments in the Pattern Library.

Basic chart for yarn calculations

The number of stitches per 18 inch length have been assessed by working Florentine stitch, Method 1. (See page 12). You will work less stitches where patterns include satin stitch blocks as in the curvature patterns.

Yarn	Yardage per skein or ball	Canvas size	Needle size	No. of stitches, over four threads, back two – for an 18 inch yarn length
Peri-Lusta Persian 3-ply	40 yards or 8.8 yards	14 threads to the inch, single canvas	18	26
Using only 2 of the above 3-ply		16 threads to the inch, single canvas	18	28
Using only 1 of the above 3-ply		24 threads to the inch, single canvas	22	50
D.M.C. Tapestry Wool	8.8 yards	16 threads to the inch, single canvas	18	28
Pearl Cotton for Linen		16 threads to the inch, single canvas	18	Used double – 24
D.M.C. Heavy Embroidery Yarn	23 yards	Double thrums canvas, 7 holes to the inch	Rug or heavy embroidery	13
Peri-Lusta 6-strand Filo		24 threads to the inch, single canvas	20	45

Needles

Tapestry needles are blunt-ended and have a wide, easily threaded eye. Any one stitch in Florentine embroidery is worked into the same hole as that on the previous row, and a pointed needle would split the stitch, blur the pattern and make a frustrating tangle of yarns. Needle sizes vary from a coarse 18 to a fine 24. 18 or 20 will be the right size for most tapestry yarns. Adjust the needle size to the yarn and canvas size. The ground threads of the canvas should not be forced out of shape by the thickness of either the yarn or needle.

To frame or not?

An embroidery frame for Florentine embroidery is a matter of personal choice. Technically, the embroidery can be evenly stitched whether held in the hand or mounted in a frame. If a frame is used, it should be a frame, not a hoop.

The frame has a circular bar at each end and a flat bar at each side. Webbing is nailed to the top and bottom bars; and the flat side bars have a series of holes for adjustment to the length of the canvas. Webbing width varies from 12 inches to about 30 inches. It must be of sufficient width to take the canvas without folding at the sides. Extra length can be rolled around the top and bottom bars and adjusted during working.

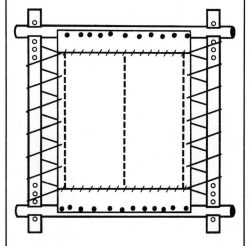

Framing the Canvas.
1. Machine stitch a wide tape over the side edges of the canvas.
2. Make a single fold at the top and bottom.
3. Match the center mark of the canvas with the center of the top roller of the frame.
4. Stitch from the center outward and overcast the canvas to the webbing.
5. Repeat for the opposite end.
6. Insert the side slats and secure with the split pins or wooden screws provided. The canvas should be taut.

7. Thread a long length of fine string into a Heavy Embroidery Needle. Working from the center of the side slats and the center of the string, lace the canvas to the side slats.
8. When both sides are threaded, pull evenly so that the canvas threads are perfectly horizontal and vertical. Tie the string to the frame. If the canvas slackens during working, untie the string and tighten from the center outward.

Working methods

Preparing the canvas. An allowance for blocking and making is included in the instructions for each piece of embroidery. When working with the canvas unframed, machine stitch a seam binding around the edge or bind the edges with masking tape. Frayed edges quickly reduce the overall size of a coarse canvas.

A large piece of canvas is easier to handle if the end not in use is rolled and fastened with a string. However simple the design may be, some guide lines basted on to the canvas are helpful both while working and when making the finished embroidery. Baste center lines horizontally and vertically, and measure and baste a line to indicate the shape of the finished piece. Count and mark the high points of a pattern where the repeat is the same throughout.

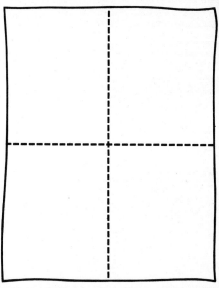

Preparing the yarns. Working with several, closely related tones of one color can cause problems. But a few simple precautions will help to keep the color sequence correct. Each skein, with its manufacturer's color number on the paper band, should be kept intact. Lay out the skeins in color order and with the color number uppermost.

Work with the skeins laid out in the same color order for the whole of any one piece of embroidery.

To remove the yarn without removing the band, pull the longer end left by the manufacturer. If, as sometimes happens, it is not immediately obvious which is the long end, pull the end from inside the skein, not the end showing outside.

Stitch structure

Simple stitches are the root of the wealth of pattern and color in Florentine embroidery. These diagrams show several ways of working stitches over four threads of the canvas. It is also possible to work the stitches over a varied number of threads. The needle positions will remain the same. Dotted lines indicate the angle of the stitch on the reverse of the canvas.

Satin stitch is a basic, flat stitch. It is repeated over the same number of threads in a straight row and the appearance on the back of the work is similar to that on the front. The curvature patterns include small groups of satin stitch worked in steps and referred to in the text as "stepped satin".

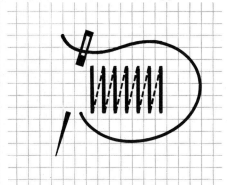

Brick stitch. This is a slightly different method of working, but has the same appearance as the two Florentine methods. It is a useful stitch for quickly covering a large area of one color.

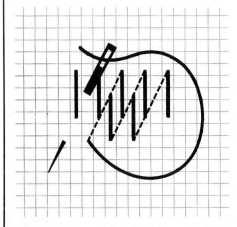

Traditional Florentine stitch. Used for many of the pattern areas, its special mark is the fluid, broken appearance where colors interlock.

Method 1. This uses comparatively little yarn, as a small slanting stitch is all that is seen on the reverse. The needle alternates between working from the top downward and the bottom upward. When working a

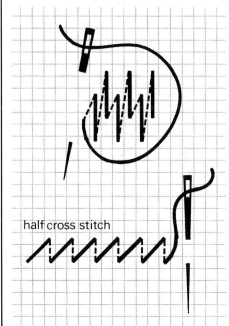

half cross stitch

pattern, make two movements of the needle for each stitch. Change the direction of the needle after a high point stitch.

Method 2. This uses more thread, with the alternating long stitch on the reverse. Mock variations of Florentine patterns can be worked in half cross-stitch.

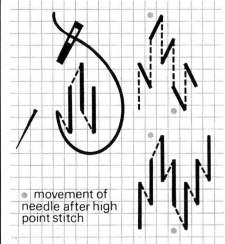

● movement of needle after high point stitch

Stitch into pattern

The patterns develop from the basic flat stitches shown. They are grouped in varying ways to make either sharp or gentle curves and angles, as described on page 6. Curves are an illusion made up from groups of stitches in angular steps. The diagram *right* shows curves and angles worked over four threads and back two. Any one piece of embroidery may use several methods of grouping. Once the basic idea is clear, the embroideries are easily worked, however complex they may appear at first glance.

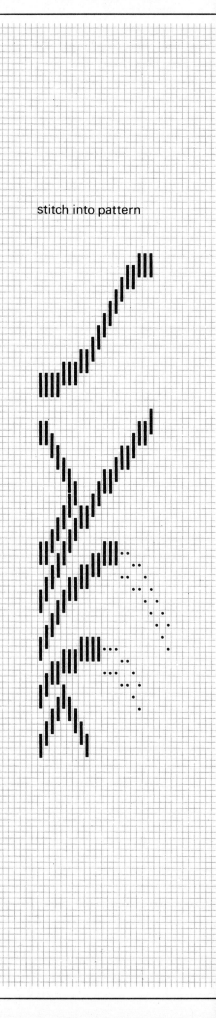

stitch into pattern

Stitching notes

To begin:

Cut a length of yarn – about 16 to 18 inches is a good working length. Leave a few inches hanging from the skein, ready for easy pulling to the next piece. Thread the needle so that the off-standing hairs of yarn are with the direction of stitching. Run a hand lightly along the yarn. In one direction the hairs lie flatter than the other. This is the direction in which to stitch for easy untangled working.

Fastening on and off:

Knot one end of the yarn. Put the needle in at the front of the canvas two or three inches from the position of the first stitch. Bring the needle up from the back and work the first few stitches. Cut off the knot, thread the end into a needle and slip the yarn through the back of the worked stitches, adding a small back stitch to secure. The next length of yarn can be threaded into the back of the previously worked stitches. Avoid fastening on and off in the same place. The extra thick stitching may show on the front.

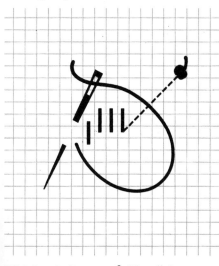

Which stitch to use? The slight texture differences between the two Florentine methods and Brick stitch disappear when the work is finished and blocked. Brick stitch is a quick working method for a large area of one color.

The foundation row. All the patterns, whether flame, zig-zag or curved, depend on an accurate foundation. In some, the whole of the embroidery is worked above and below one foundation row; in others, each section or motif is filled in from one outer foundation row. Once this row has been laid, the rest follows almost automatically. A helpful aid to correct counting of threads is to stitch the foundation row in two movements. If the embroidery is being worked in the hand and not in a frame, the tendency is to make the stitch in one movement of the needle. Try making it in two – that is, put it in at the front and take it out from the back putting it into the next position from the back. Repeat from the front. Working in this way, the threads are more clearly seen for counting. If mistakes are made, be ruthless and cut them out! To unpick takes longer, and yarn gets so worn and rubbed from being pulled back through the canvas that it is impossible to use it again.

How to work from a chart using a base line

Many of the patterns built up from one base line repeat their curves or angles in such a way that they may be started at any point on the canvas. The tones repeat above and below the base line and can be fitted with half stitches into the outline of the article being worked, with little noticeable difference as to where the pattern begins or ends. **Symmetry.** For square or oblong pillows, or any embroideries in which symmetry is needed, begin at the marked center lines on the canvas. Stitch the first row from the center outward. The next rows may be stitched straight across, beginning at the point on the chart which the end of the row has reached. As you work the base line, check back on the number of stitches.

If you have two where there should have been one, this may not show in the early stages but will upset the balance over the completed embroidery. Check again when the row is complete. Follow on with the colors in the order given. If your base line is accurate, there is no need to count again.

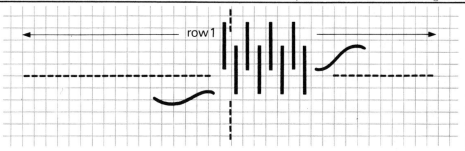

working from a base line

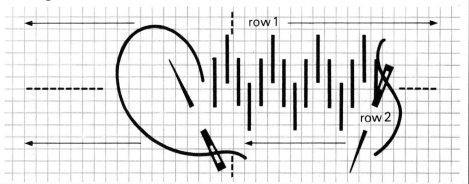

Drawing a pattern onto canvas

Use this method for any shaped patterns to which you wish to adapt your Florentine work, such as the curtain tie-back and vest, on pages 41 and 55. Onto paper (old newspaper will do), draw the outline required in thick black felt pen. For garments like the vest, it is best to work from a bought pattern. For the tie-back, enlarge the given outline. Position the canvas on the paper or commercial pattern. Match the straight of the pattern with the straight weave of the canvas. The thickly drawn or printed line is easily seen through the canvas. Pencil or baste outline onto the canvas. Work the embroidery up to the outline. Cut out when the embroidery is finished. See diagram *right*.

Measuring canvas for chairs and stools

To measure the canvas size needed for all-over embroidery for a chair seat, footstool or fender stool, first remove the old seat cover. Smooth out the shapings, leaving the seam allowance turned in. Cut a paper pattern; and onto it, mark any shapings such as mitered corners. This will be the area which the embroidery will need to cover. Measure at least two inches at each side beyond the furthest extent of the shaping. This is the size of canvas required. Draw the outline onto canvas as shown on page 13. Do not cut any shaping until the finishing process.

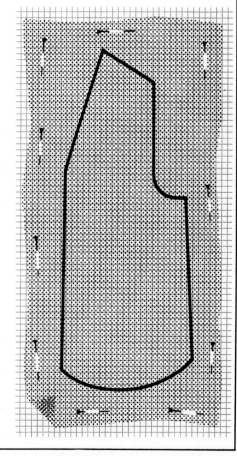

patterns
galore

Left A wonderful array of colorful pillows. Detailed instructions, shade numbers and graphs for most of these patterns are given in the comprehensive Pattern Library which follows on pages 16-27—the rest are covered in the introduction. Mix or match designs: clash or complement your colors. Start with the simpler repeated shapes. Then work your way through, as you master each scheme, to the fascinatingly intricate carnation—the ultimate in Florentine stitchery. (The one pillow for which detailed instructions are not given is the patchwork one.)

Gothic

A horizontal pattern with curvature and flame patterns combining to dramatic effect. The design is worked over six canvas threads and back three. The exaggerated curve is formed by working over these six threads instead of four as in the Romanesque pattern.

Peri-Lusta colors: 1. 455 white; **2.** 139 apricot; **3.** 138; **4.** 137; **5.** 804 orange; **6.** 803; **7.** 802; **8.** 801; **9.** 706 red; **10.** 707 flame; **11.** 708 salmon; **12.** 709 pink.
One repeat = S. 87 / W.6¾″ / H. 4½″ / Y. 1 yd. 24″.
For key to abbreviations, see page 10.

With D.M.C. Tapestry: 12 colors to your choice. Width, height and yardage will be marginally smaller than with Peri-Lusta yarn over one repeat, due to difference in canvas size. (See chart on page 11).

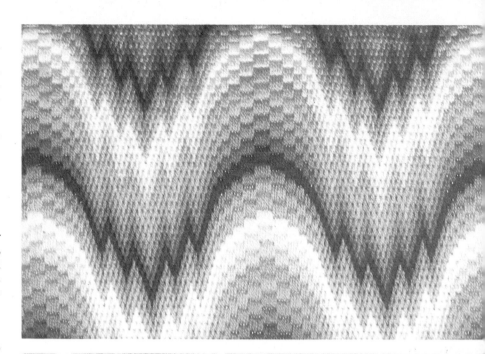

Romanesque

A horizontal pattern with white between two dark tones for sharp contrast, and worked over four canvas threads and back two. The pattern combines a simple zigzag with a curvature design.

Peri-Lusta colors: 1. 455 white; **2.** 805 aubergine; **3.** 303; **4.** 304; **5.** 305; **6.** 306; **7.** 159 clover; **8.** 160; **9.** 161; **10.** 183 pink; **11.** 182; **12.** 181.
One repeat = S. 73 / W. 5½″ / H. 2¾″ / Y. 1½ yds.
For key to abbreviations, see page 10.

With D.M.C. Tapestry: 12 colors to your choice. Width, height and yardage will be marginally smaller than with Peri-Lusta yarn over one repeat, due to difference in canvas size. (See chart on page 11).

Pomegranate

This pomegranate or ogee design is worked over four canvas threads, back two. Stitch the horizontal curvature pattern across the canvas in color **1.** Stitch a second row, reversed across the canvas, in the same color. Fill in the resulting ogee shape with the color sequence shown on the chart.

Peri-Lusta colors: 1. 804 orange; **2.** 803; **3.** 802; **4.** 801; **5.** 706 red; **6.** 285 black; **7.** 455 white; **8.** 292 lemon.

One repeat = S. 46 (color **1.**): Y. 41″
                     43 (color **2.**):   39″
                     41 (color **3.**):   37″
                     39 (color **4.**):   36″
                     35 (color **5.**):   31″
                     27 (color **6.**):   19″
                     19 (color **7.**):   14″
                     18 (color **8.**):   13″
            W. 3½″ / H. 3¾″.
For key to abbreviations, see page 10.

With D.M.C. Tapestry: 8 colors to your choice. Width, height and yardage will be marginally smaller than with Peri-Lusta yarn over one repeat, due to difference in canvas size. (See chart on page 11).

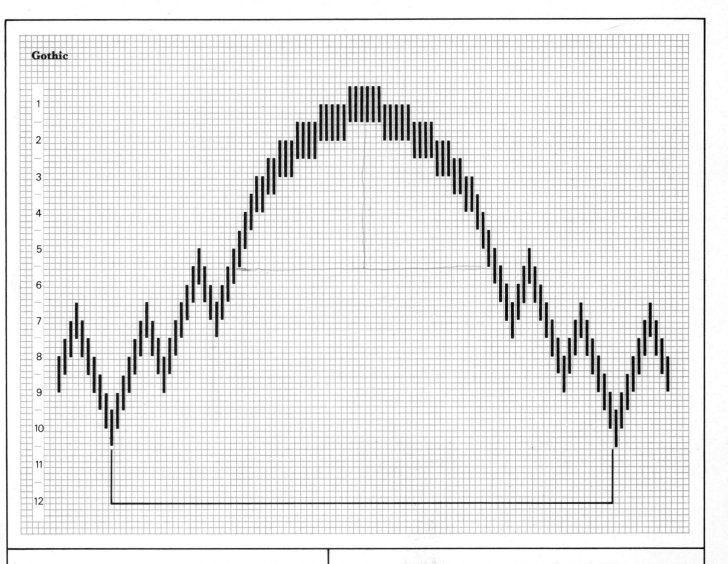

Gothic

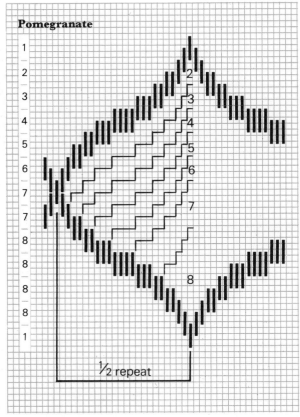

Pomegranate

½ repeat

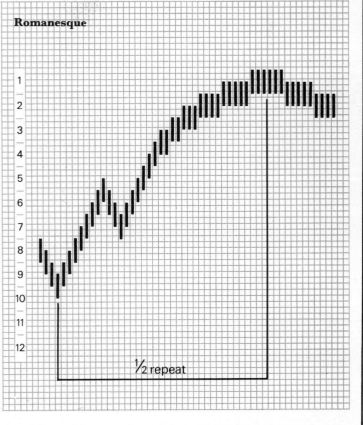

Romanesque

½ repeat

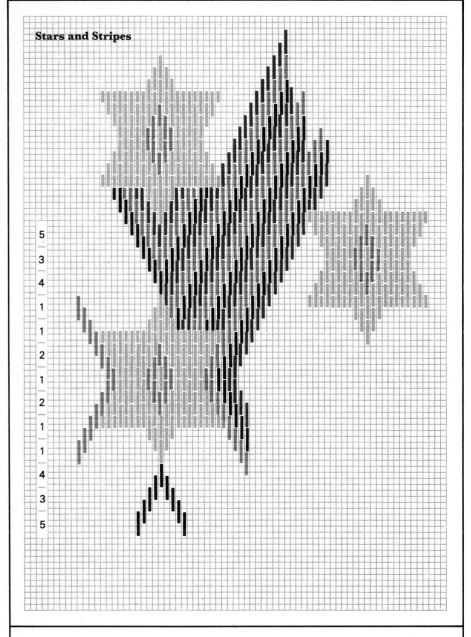

Stars and Stripes

Stars and Stripes

A design worked over four canvas threads, back two. The stripes radiate from a central star. Mark the vertical and horizontal centers of the canvas. Work the first white star with its center stitch at the center threads of the canvas. Complete the star and radiate the blue lines from it in the color sequence shown on the chart.

Peri-Lusta colors: 1. 455 white: **2.** 252 pale blue; **3.** 250 mid-blue; **4.** 247 navy blue; **5.** 399 turquoise.
The star = S. 76 (color **1.**): Y. 1 yd. 18″
        8 (color **2.**): Y. 1 yd. 6″
        W. 1½″ / H. 2″.
1 yard will work 52 stitches in the background diagonal.
For key to abbreviations, see page 10.

With D.M.C. Tapestry: 5 colors to your choice. Width, height and yardage will be marginally smaller than with Peri-Lusta yarn over one repeat, due to difference in canvas size. (See chart on page 11).

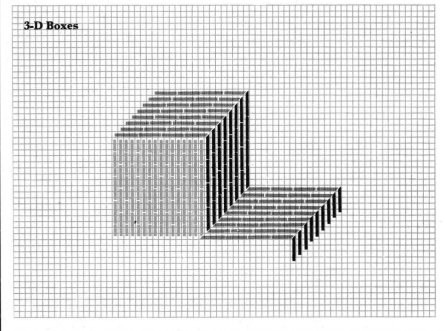

3-D Boxes

3-D Boxes

Each box is worked in three tones of one color, over four threads and back two; and over four threads, back three. A light tone for the four/two stitching on the face of the box contrasts with two darker tones in two directions of four/three stitching. Note that where the colors meet, four stitches enter the same hole. Colors: an experimental range of three tones of one color for each box.

With Peri-Lusta yarn:
One box = S. 61 (light tone): Y. 1 yd 7″
        32 (medium tone): 22″
        32 (dark tone): 22″
        W.1¾″ / H. 1¾″.
For key to abbreviations, see page 10.

With D.M.C. Tapestry: 3 shades of one color to your choice for each box. Width, height and yardage will be marginally smaller than with Peri-Lusta yarn over one repeat, due to difference in canvas size. (See chart on page 11).

Honeycomb

Work this design over four canvas threads, back two. Satin stitch blocks and diagonal lines make the honeycomb outline in color **5.** A sequence of satin stitch and diagonal lines fill the outline. The satin stitch blocks are worked one below another. Keep the stitch tension loose in order to cover the canvas.

Peri-Lusta colors: 1. 455 white; **2.** 139 orange/red; **3.** 138; **4.** 137; **5.** 136.
One repeat = S. 35 (honeycomb outline): 19 (color **4.**): 17 (color **3.**): 28 (color **2.**): 27 (color **1.**) / W. $1\frac{3}{4}''$ / H. $2\frac{1}{3}''$ / Y. 27″ (honeycomb outline): 13″ (color **4.**): 13″ (color **3.**): 20″ (color **2.**): 19″ (color **1.**)
For key to abbreviations, see page 10.

With D.M.C. Tapestry: 5 colors to your choice. Width, height and yardage will be marginally smaller than with Peri-Lusta yarn over one repeat, due to difference in canvas size. (See chart on page 11).

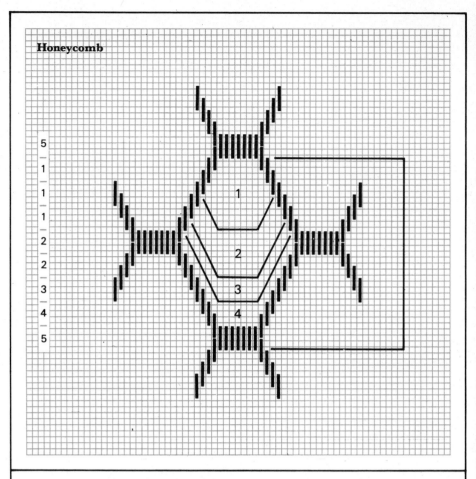

Trellis Major

An interesting, interlacing trellis which needs close concentration to establish the basic lines. Begin with a white diamond and build up the color lines outward. The design is worked over four threads and back two. Thread several needles with the color sequence and work a few stitches of each color until you have laid the bones of the design correctly. Begin at the vertical center of the canvas and work outward.

Peri-Lusta colors: 1. 709 pale orange; **2.** 643 clear coral pink; **3.** 642 coral pink; **4.** 485 dark coral pink; **5.** 803 mid-orange; **6.** 707 dark orange; **7.** 113 donkey brown; **8.** 121 dark brown; **9.** 455 white.
One repeat = S. 22 (diagonal line from one interlace to the next): 25 (white diamond): 11, 13 and 15 (white diamond shadow) / W. 2″ / H.4″ / Y. 18″ (diagonal line): 18″ (white diamond): 9″ (colors **1.** and **7.**, white diamond shadow): 12″ (color **8.**, white diamond shadow).
For key abbreviations, see page 10.

With D.M.C. Tapestry: 9 colors to your choice. Width, height and yardage will be marginally smaller than with Peri-Lusta yarn over one repeat, due to difference in canvas size. (See chart on page 11).

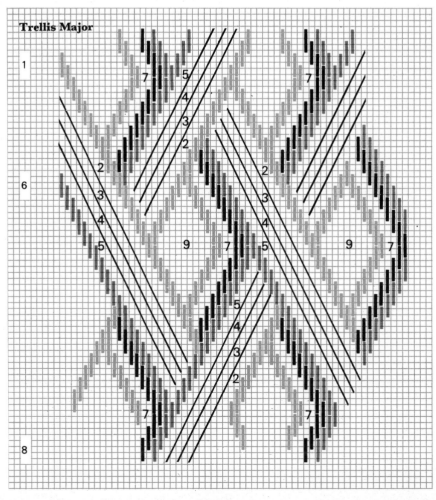

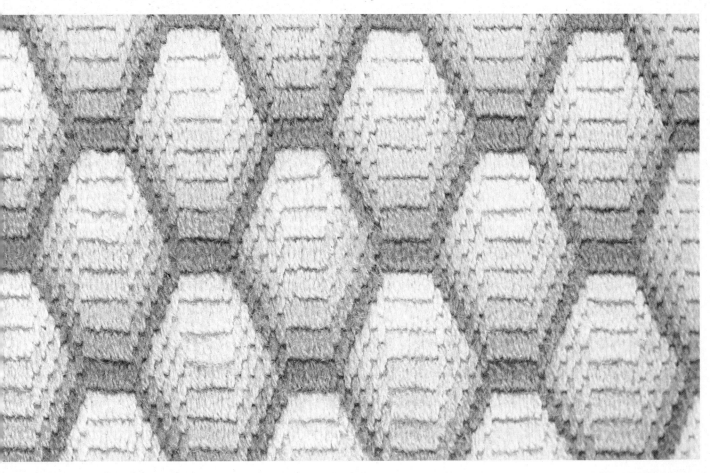

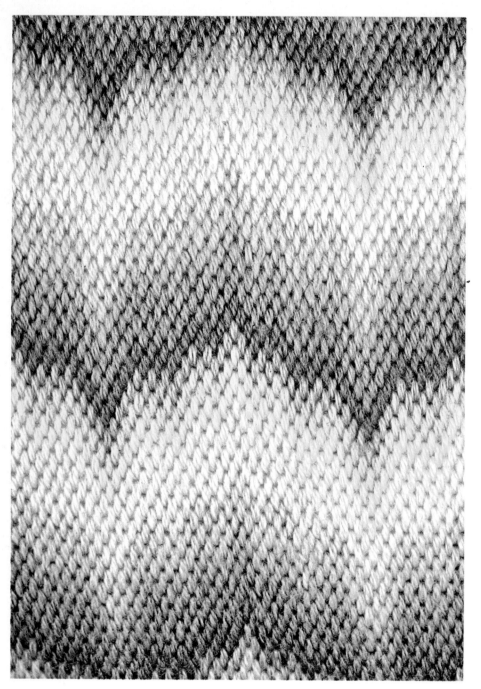
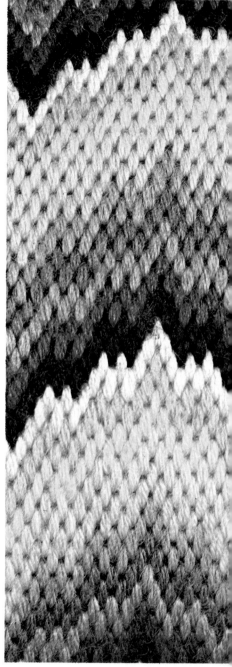

Aurora Borealis

Two horizontal designs with base line identical, worked over four canvas threads and back two. A different effect has been achieved in Design B by the sharp contrast which white gives between two very dark tones. In Design A, there is a continuous progression of tone from light to dark, and dark to light again.

Peri-Lusta colors: Design A. **1.** 711 dark green; **2.** 712; **3.** 713; **4.** 819; **5.** 714; **6.** 440 pale green; **7.** 455 white; **8.** 295 pale yellow; **9.** 705 mid-yellow; **10.** 375 gold/green; **11.** 292 deep gold/green; **12.** 276 honey.
Design B. **1.** 455 white; **2.** 442 gold; **3.** 443; **4.** 444; **5.** 445; **6.** 276 honey; **7.** 275 cinnamon; **8.** 218 pale gray; **9.** 217 mid-gray; **10.** 285 black.
One repeat = S. 28 / W. 3″ / H. 1¾″ / Y. 27″.

22

With D.M.C. Tapestry: 10 or 12 colors to your choice. Width, height and yardage will be marginally smaller than with Peri-Lusta yarn over one repeat, due to difference in canvas size. (See chart on page 11). For key to abbreviations, see page 10.

Fountain Brocade

A design worked over six canvas threads, back two. It is a much easier pattern to work than its appearance suggests. It is a continuous horizontal pattern with alternate steps of long and short stitches. Pale lemon alternates with every color row, breaking the steady flow of the color sequence. The pale lemon row forms a narrow line: the blocks over two threads of canvas alternate with a single long stitch over six threads. The color sequence is from seaweed through lemon to dark orange, reversing back again to seaweed.

Peri-Lusta colors: 1. 275 seaweed; **2.** 296 pale lemon; **3.** 442 dark gold; **4.** 443 gold; **5.** 444 pale gold; **6.** 804 pale orange; **7.** 803 orange; **8.** 802 mid-orange; **9.** 801 dark orange.
Each horizontal repeat = S. 35 / W. 2½″ / H. 3″ / Y. 18″ (for wide repeat in bold shades): 11″ (for narrow repeat in pale lemon).
For key abbreviations, see page 10.

With D.M.C. Tapestry: 9 colors to your choice. Width, height and yardage will be marginally smaller than with Peri-Lusta yarn over one repeat, due to difference in canvas size. (See chart on page 11).

*Above Designs A and B for
Aurora Borealis.
Right Fountain Brocade.*

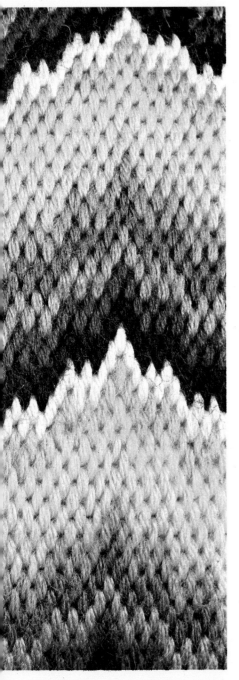

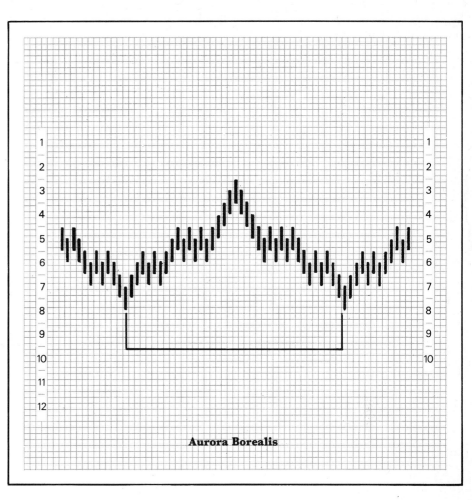

Aurora Borealis

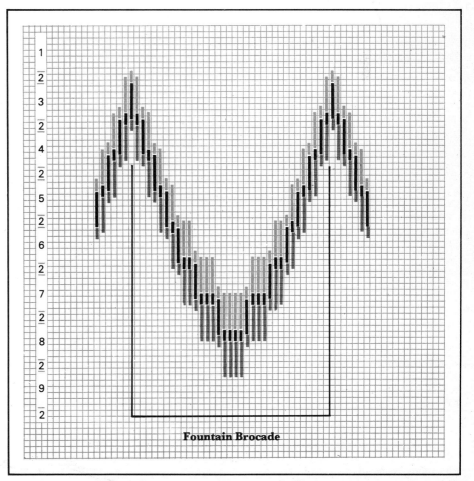

Fountain Brocade

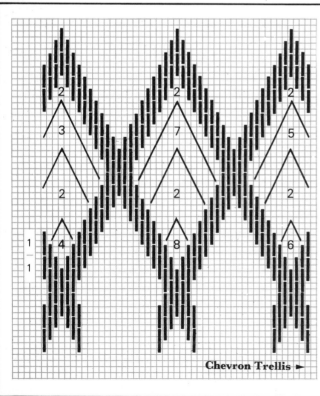

Chevron Trellis ▶

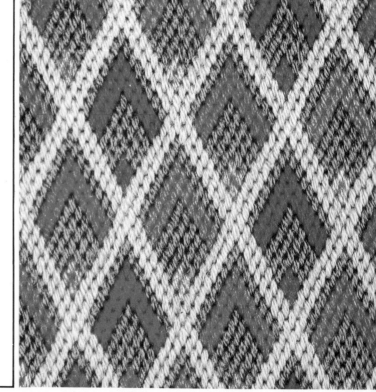

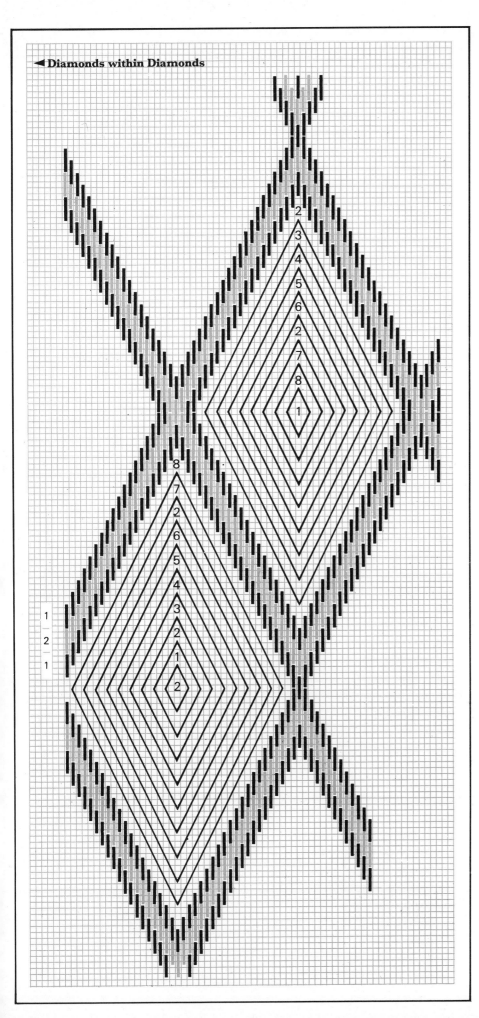

◄ Diamonds within Diamonds

Diamonds within Diamonds

A simple reversed zigzag pattern with a trellis row in white stitching between. The color sequence is light to dark, reversing between the zigzag rows. Work a zigzag black row horizontally, a white trellis row, then the reversed black zigzag. Fill in the sequence of colors as shown on the chart.

Peri-Lusta colors: 1. 285 black; **2.** 455 white; **3.** 704 puce; **4.** 703; **5.** 702; **6.** 701; **7.** 258 pale pink; **8.** 257 dark pink.
One diamond repeat = S.84 (outline). Each subsequent row within the outline decreases by 8 stitches / W. 3¼″ / H. 6″ / Y. 1 yd. 22″. Reduce your calculation by about 4 inches for each subsequent color row within the outline.
For key abbreviations, see page 10.

With D.M.C. Tapestry: 8 colors to your choice. Width, height and yardage will be marginally smaller than with Peri-Lusta yarn over one repeat, due to difference in canvas size. (See chart on page 11).

Chevron Trellis

This pattern is worked over four threads and back two. Work the two row trellis in green, and fill in the resulting diamonds with the three-color chevron centers. For these, there are three different color combinations against the dark green ground. The same colors are in vertical rows but alternate diagonally and horizontally.

Peri-Lusta colors: 1. 713 pale green; **2.** 817 emerald; **3.** 180 dark pink; **4.** 181 pale pink; **5.** 224 dark red; **6.** 225 red; **7.** 707 orange; **8.** 708 coral.
One single row trellis repeat = S. 36 (color **2.**); 26 (chevron): 4 (small diamond) / W. 1¼″ / H. 2¾″ / Y. ½yd. (color **2.**): 18″ (chevron): 3″ (small diamond).
For key to abbreviations, see page 10.

With D.M.C. Tapestry: 8 colors to your choice. Width, height and yardage will be marginally smaller than with Peri-Lusta yarn over one repeat, due to difference in canvas size. (See chart on page 11).

26

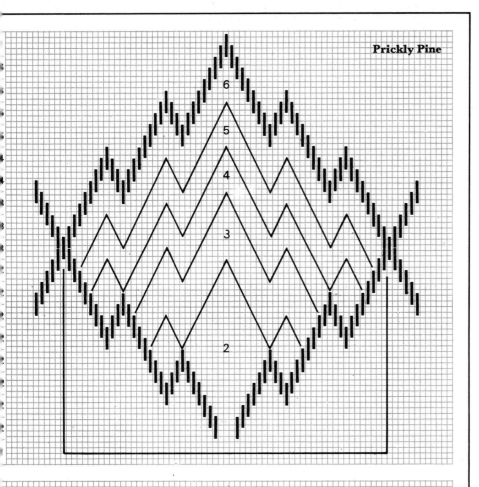

Prickly Pine

Prickly Pine

This design is worked over four canvas threads, back two. For the outline, work a reversed row so that the stitch where the lines meet serves as the center stitch for both. Fill in the resulting shape with the color sequence as shown on the chart.

Peri-Lusta colors: 1. 805 dark aubergine; **2.** 833 pale turquoise; **3.** 832; **4.** 831; **5.** 830; **6.** 159 clover pink.

One repeat = S. 60 (color **1.**):Y. 1yd. 6″
           116 (color **2.**):   2yds. 9″
           104 (color **3.**):   2yds.
           88 (color **4.**):   1yd. 26″
           70 (color **5.**):   1yd. 14″
           64 (color **6.**):   1yd. 9″
       W. 4½″ / H. 5″.

For key to abbreviations, see page 10.

With D.M.C. Tapestry: 6 colors to your choice. Width, height and yardage will be marginally smaller than with Peri-Lusta yarn over one repeat, due to difference in canvas size. (See chart on page 11).

Carnations

A series of zigzag and diamond patterns within a variously shaped outline, worked over four canvas threads, back two. Work an outline in the background color. Then, within this outline, work each section step by step, starting at the high point and working outward.

Peri-Lusta colors: 1. 703 shocking pink; **2.** 304 pale aubergine; **3.** 303 dark aubergine; **4.** 161 palest mushroom; **5.** 258 pale pink; **6.** 257 dark pink; **7.** 426 mauve; **8.** 427 mid-purple; **9.** 425 dark purple; **10.** 723 dark turquoise; **11.** 833 turquoise; **12.** 713 background green.

One carnation motif = S. 205 (color **12.**, outline), 194 (color **1.**), 78 (color **2.**), 69 (color **3.**), 102 (color **4.**), 100 (color **5.**), 50 (color **6.**), 72 (color **7.**), 16 (color **8.**), 41 (color **9.**), 57 (color **10.**), 54 (color **11.**) / W. 6½″ / H. 5¾″.

Y. 4 yards of color **12** for outline.

For filling in the background (1 yard = 52 stitches): 3yds. 27″ (color **1.**), 1yd. 18″ (color **2.**), 1yd. 13″ (color **3.**), 2yds. (color **4.**), 2yds. (color **5.**), 1yd. (color **6.**), 1yd. 15″ (color **7.**), 14″ (color **8.**), 27″ (color **9.**), 1yd. 4″ (color **10.**), 1yd. 2″ (color **11.**).

For key to abbreviations, see page 10.

With D.M.C. Tapestry: 12 colors to your choice. Width, height and yardage will be marginally smaller than with Peri-Lusta yarn over one repeat, due to difference in canvas size. (See chart on page 11).

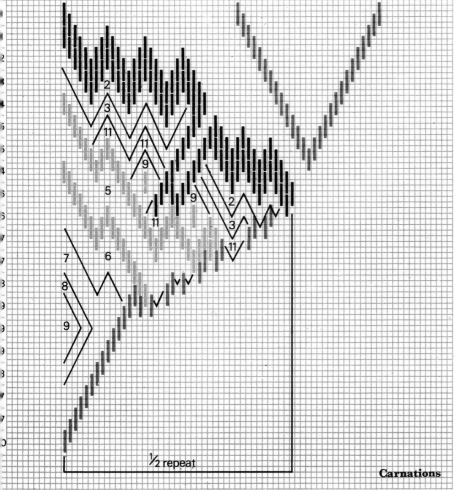

½ repeat

Carnations

florentine designs

This magnificent sampler rug, worked in a dazzling variety of Florentine patterns, heralds a section devoted to Florentine designs. Belts and bags, pillows and chair covers, a vest and a wallhanging—you'll find a host of wonderful ideas for using finished work. Two spreads of fabulous fashion designs have also been included: while instructions for finishing follow in the section starting on page 60.

little gifts

Five miniature Florentine designs—easy to work, attractive and useful.

Three designs which look like Florentine but which are worked in half cross-stitch are included here. (See page 12). The color range for all the embroideries is as follows: D.M.C. Tapestry Wool. **1.** 7599; **2.** 7314; **3.** 7708; **4.** 7547; **5.** 7797.

For each object, you will need one skein in each color. For longer belts, more yarn may be required.

Hairband (mock Florentine)
Finished measurement: 9½″ x 1½″.
Fabric: Single canvas, 16 threads to the inch, 11″ x 3″. Lining, 11″ x 3″.
Elastic: Short length, ¾″ wide.
Needle: Tapestry, No. 18.
Stitch: Half cross-stitch.

Work in half cross-stitch with the colors indicated on the chart. Repeat the pattern until the embroidery measures 9½ inches long. Block and make as on page 60.

Clasp belt (mock Florentine)
Finished measurement: About 2″ x required length.
Fabric: Double canvas, 10 holes to inch, 6″ x required length. Lining, 6″ x required length. Bought buckle.
Needle: Tapestry, No. 18.
Stitch: Half cross-stitch.

Work in half cross-stitch and following the pattern on the chart. Repeat the pattern until the desired length has been worked. Allow extra length for the overlap through the buckle. Finish as on page 61.

Lighter case (mock Florentine)
Finished measurement: 2¾″ x 2½″.
Fabric: Double canvas, 10 holes to the inch, 9″ x 5″. Lining, 9″ x 5″. 12″ of fine cord.
Needle: Tapestry, No. 18.
Stitch: Half cross-stitch.

Follow the chart for pattern and color and fill in an area 2¾″ x 5″. Block and make as on page 60.

Glasses case
Finished measurement: 6½″ x 2¾″.
Fabric: Single canvas, 16 threads to the inch, 19″ x 7″. Lining, 19″ x 7″. 24″ of fine cord.
Needle: Tapestry, No. 18.
Stitch: Florentine.

Work over four canvas threads and back two, following the colors and pattern shown on the chart. Repeat until the embroidery measures 14½″ x 2¾″. Block and make as on page 60.

Compact case
Finished measurement: 3¾″ x 3¾″.
Fabric: Single canvas, 16 threads to the inch, 11″ x 7″. Lining, 11″ x 7″. 12″ of fine cord.
Needle: Tapestry, No. 18.
Stitch: Florentine

Work the pattern across the canvas in the colors indicated. Repeat for 7½″. Block and make as shown on page 60.

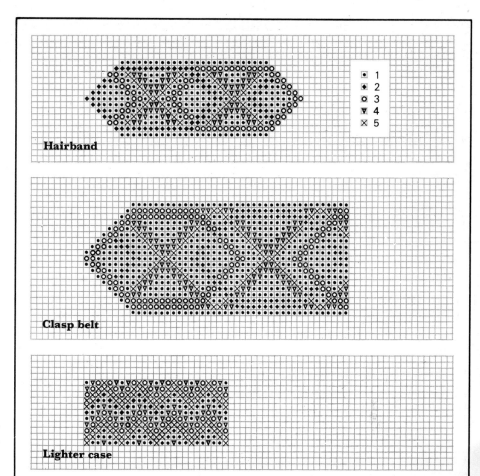

Hairband

Clasp belt

Lighter case

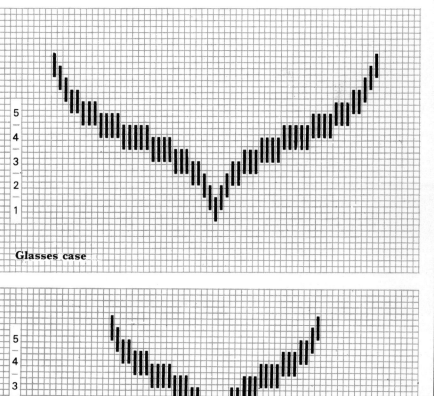

Glasses case

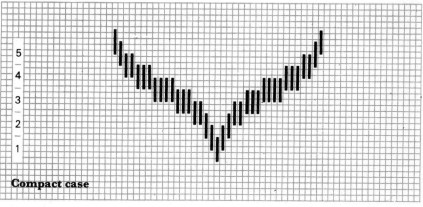

Compact case

Finished measurement: About 12″ x 9″.
Fabric: Single canvas, 24 threads to the inch, 28″ x 16″. Matching linen for gussets, 15″ x 10″. Lining for handbag and gusset, about 1 yard of 36″ fabric. Pellon or similar non-woven interlining, about 27″ x 36″.
Yarn: Work the bag in 6-strand floss using seven colors. We have chosen the following.
1. white
2. pale gray
3. almond green
4. amber gold
5. gold
6. chestnut
7. muscat green
Needle: Tapestry, No. 22.
Stitch: Satin.
A large snap fastener.

florentine flap~over

Accessorize Florentine style, with this colorful but neat evening clutch.

Mark out the canvas as indicated on the diagram. Working from the chart (using all 6 strands of Embroidery floss), begin at the center point and work the bag flap as indicated. The stitch is taken over 8 threads and back 6. Continue working the seven color repeat over the sequence of eleven rows for the remainder of the bag. Make a trial fold and adjust the extent of the embroidery so that the pattern on the front flap matches that of the front fold of the bag – about 72 rows of stitching. Finish on the final row with half stitches where necessary. Backstitch a row in medium color to make the edge of the finished embroidery neat. Block, line and finish as on page 61.

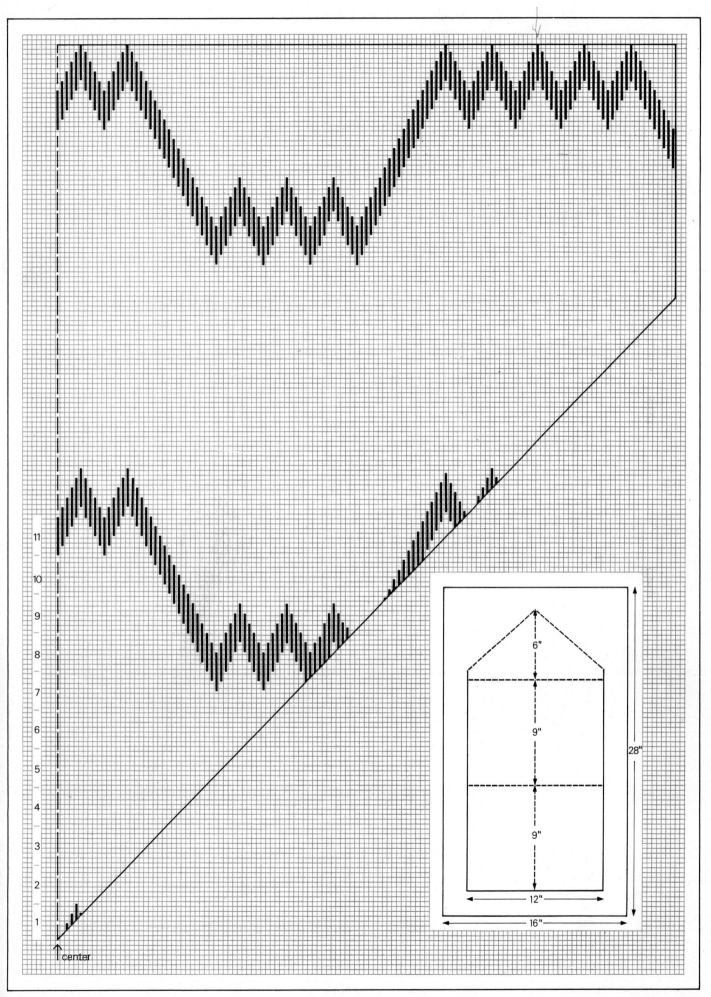

bargello pillows – plain and patchwork

Plain pillows

Finished measurement: About 10½″ x 17″.

Fabric: Double thrums canvas, 7 holes to the inch, 14″ x 21″ for each pillow. Woolen fabric for backing, 12″ x 19″ for each pillow.

Yarn: D.M.C. Heavy Embroidery Yarn in the following colors.

For Pillow 1. **1.** jonquil; **2.** lime; **3.** cedar green; **4.** cypress green.

For Pillow 2. **1.** jonquil; **2.** copper; **3.** nasturtium; **4.** snapdragon.

For Pillow 3. **1.** snapdragon; **2.** poppy; **3.** oleander; **4.** true blue.

For Pillow 4. **1.** jonquil; **2.** copper **3.** tobacco; **4.** brown.

Needle: Rug or heavy embroidery with blunt point.

Stitch: Florentine, Method 1. (See page 12). Mark the horizontal and vertical centers of the canvas. For the embroidery, mark the oblong 10½″ x 17″. All four of the pillows are worked to the same pattern.

Begin at the centers with color **1.** and work across the canvas. Follow on, row by row in the color sequence given. Where needed, work half stitches to finish at the outline of the pillow. Block and finish as shown on page 60.

Patchwork Pillows

Finished measurements: Each square of the two background pillows measures about 5½″ x 5½″. The overall measurement of each pillow is about 16½″ x 16½″. Each square of the foreground pillow measures about 6″ x 6″, and the complete pillow 18″ x 18″. Add more squares to make handsome floor pillows.

Fabric: Double thrums canvas, 7 holes to the inch. (Allow 1½″ outside each square of embroidery for blocking and finishing.) Wool fabric for backing. (Allow 1″ all around for turnings.)

Yarn: D.M.C. Heavy Embroidery Yarn in the following colors.

For Pillow 1. **1.** nasturtium; **2.** poppy **3.** snapdragon.

For Pillow 2. **1.** white; **2.** light red **3.** black.

For Pillow 3. **1.** white; **2.** copper; **3.** light red.

Needle: Rug or heavy embroidery needle with blunt point.

Stitch: Florentine, Method 1.(See page 12).

For Pillow 1. Work over six threads and back three. Mark the centers of each canvas square and baste or draw in the 6 inch area. Begin at one end and work across in the simple Florentine pattern. The color sequence repeats throughout in numbers **1.**, **2.** and **3.** Work the number of squares required. Block and finish as shown on page 60. Note that the squares are stitched together vertically and horizontally.

For Pillow 2. Work over four threads and back two. Mark the centers of each square and outline the 5½ inch area. The alternate squares are worked in two arrangements of color. Work four squares from Chart A and five squares from Chart B. Begin in each case at the left hand corner in color **3,** and work diagonally across the square. Block and finish as shown on page 60. Stitch the squares together with the Florentine stitch running in the same direction.

For Pillow 3. Work over four threads and back two as for the center pillow. Follow Chart C using the background pillow colors. The finishing is the same as for the Background Pillow: that is, the squares are stitched together alternately horizontally and vertically.

Back the pillows with a wool jersey or a similar fabric, or knit or crochet a square in matching yarn.

Block and finish as shown on page 60.

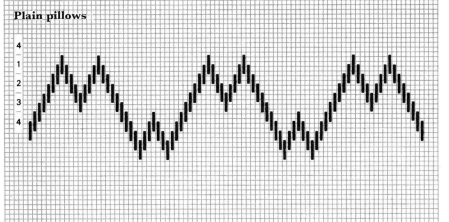

Plain pillows

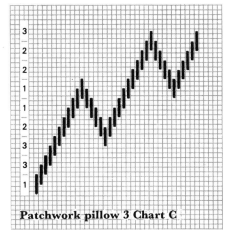

Patchwork pillow 1

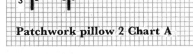

Patchwork pillow 2 Chart A

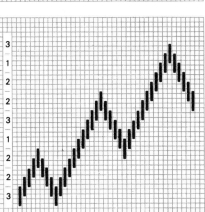

Patchwork pillow 2 Chart B

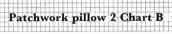

Patchwork pillow 3 Chart C

decorative strip designs

Three Florentine belts to tone or contrast; while decorative bands give that final splash of color to a flowing caftan.

Belt with 3-D cubes

Finished measurement: About 2¾″ x 28″, or adapt as required.

Fabric: Single canvas, 14 threads to the inch, 8″ x 32″ for 28 inch waist size; or adapt as required, allowing 4 inches for blocking and finishing. Lining, about 8″ x 32″ for 28 inch waist size.

Yarn: Peri-Lusta 3-ply Persian, in the following colors: one 8.8 yard skein of shades **1.**, **3.** and **4.** and three of colors **2.** and **5.**

1. 803 mid-orange; **2.** 285 black; **3.** 804 pale orange; **4.** 205 brown/orange; **5.** 135 orange.

Needle: Tapestry, No. 18.

Stitches: Brick and satin. (See page 12). Large snap fasteners.

Work the simulated buckle in one with the remainder of the belt. Mark the lengthwise center of the canvas. Work the simulated buckle first. Over four threads and back two, work a brick stitch center and one row of satin stitch in color **3.** Leave four threads and work the first of the box patterns. The color sequence for these is the same throughout. Note that the stitches are worked in two different directions: the main stitching and background down the width, and color **3.** down the length. (See Pattern Library, page 18). Complete the pattern and background, then trim the canvas to about 10 threads. Fold at four threads and overcast with satin stitch in color **1.** Finish as shown on page 61.

Zigzag belt

Finished measurement: 2″ x 28″, or adapt as required.

Fabric: Single canvas, 14 threads to the inch, 7″ x 86″, for 28 inch waist size; or adapt as required, allowing 4 inches for blocking and finishing and another 4 inches to pass through the buckle. Lining, 7″ x 32″ for 28 inch waist size. Bought buckle.

Yarn: Peri-Lusta 3-ply Persian in the following colors. Two skeins of each shade. Mauve/pink range: **1.** 704; **2.** 702; **3.** 306; **4.** 305; **4.** 303; **6.** 805.

Needle: Tapestry, No. 18.

Stitch: Satin.

Work the simple zigzag design over four threads and back three down the length of the canvas. Keep the tension loose, otherwise the canvas may show between the rows of stitching. Trim and finish the edge and make as for the 3-D cube belt.

Medallion belt

Finished measurement: Width, about 3″. Length, 28″ – or adapt as required.

Fabric: Single canvas, 14 threads to the inch, 10″ x 32″ for 28 inch waist size; or adapt as required, allowing 4 inches for blocking and finishing. Lining, 10″ x 32″ for 28 inch waist size.

Yarn: Peri-Lusta 3-ply Persian in the following colors. One 8.8 yard skein of each color: two of shades **8.** and **2.** Yellow range: **1.** 446; **2.** 445; **3.** 444; **4.** 443; **5.** 442; **6.** 385 pale gray; **7.** 287 charcoal gray; **8.** 285 black.

Pink/orange/red range: **9.** 256; **10.** 257;

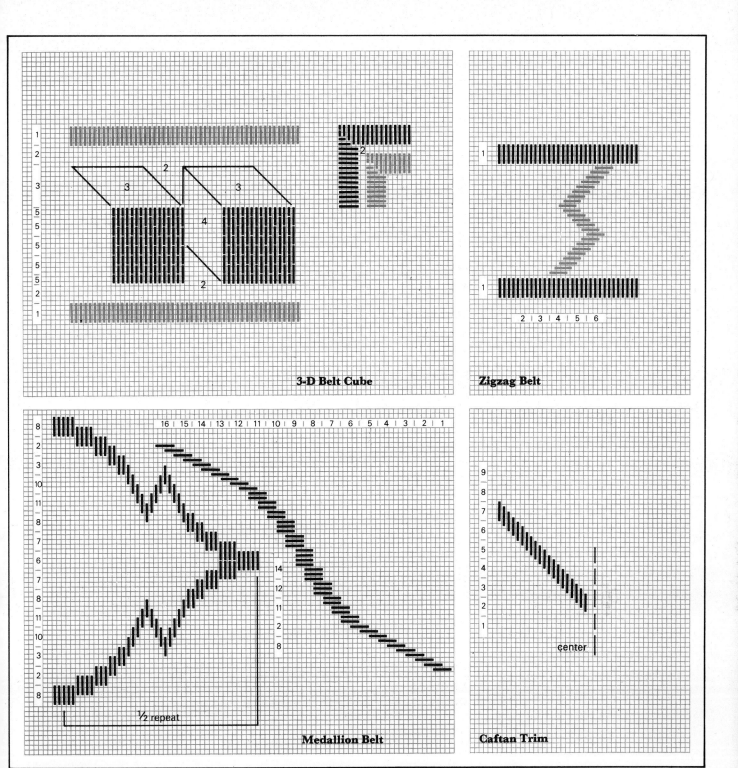

11. 258; **12.** 138; **13.** 709; **14.** 485; **15.** 707; **16.** 135.

Needle: Tapestry, No. 18.
Stitch: Florentine.
Large snap fasteners or hooks.

The back of the belt has a single medallion from which spring the opposing curvature patterns. Two medallions are worked at the front to form a "buckle". Mark the center widthwise of the belt, and work the medallion outline in black. Stitch over four threads and back two down the narrow width. Fill in the consecutive rows with the color numbers shown on the chart. The belt length is stitched in the opposite direction. Work the curvature pattern, repeating the 15 colors in sequence. Continue stitching for the desired length. Measure the finished medallion (about 6½ inches) and include another in your waist measurement. Adjust the waist measurement by lapping one of the front medallions over the other. Block and finish as shown on page 61.

Caftan trim
Finished measurement: Each diagonal stripe about 1½" wide and length as required.
Fabric: Single canvas. 14 threads to the inch, at least 10" wide and length required.
Yarn: Peri-Lusta 3-ply Persian yarn. One 8.8 yard skein in each color will work about an 18" strip of opposing diagonals.
1. 180 dark pink; **2.** 181 pale pink; **3.** 805 dark aubergine; **4.** 224 red; **5.** 706 orange; **6.** 707 orange; **7.** 225 dusty orange; **8.** 708 orange; **9.** 709 apricot.
Needle: Tapestry, No. 18.
Stitch: Stepped satin.

Mark the vertical center of the canvas and begin stitching 14 threads (one inch) to the right of this center line; and for the opposing diagonals, 14 threads to the left. There are twenty stitches in each row as shown on the base line chart. Note that the stitch is taken over four threads of the canvas and back three. This makes a stepped satin stitch. Continue in the color sequence shown until the desired length has been worked. Leave a break of two inches and continue with a second pair of diagonal bands for the trimming at the lower edge. Finish as on page 61.

quick-to -finish wallhanging

Work this exciting wall-hanging in whatever color combination you choose for a splendid touch of eastern promise. Then, why not try a matching rug too?

Finished measurement: 38″ x 24″.
Fabric: Double thrums canvas, 7 holes to the inch, 47″ x 28″.
Yarn: D.M.C. Heavy Embroidery Yarn.
1. sable brown; **2.** light chestnut; **3.** camel; **4.** light beige; **5.** white; **6.** copper; **7.** light gray; **8.** black; **9.** brown; **10.** tobacco; **11.** yellow ocher; **12.** mustard.
Needle: Rug or heavy embroidery.
Wooden batten, 20″ x 1″ x ½″.

A subtle range of tone and length of stitch combine in this design, bringing new dimensions to a simple zigzag pattern. Two inches from the lower edge of the canvas, mark out the 38″ x 24″ area. The remaining seven inches at the top will fold over to form a sleeve for the batten. Work from the base line at the lower edge. The first seven rows are worked over eight double threads of the canvas. Follow the chart carefully for the base line. The stitches are taken forward over eight threads and back three, except at each side of the high points where they are back one. The hanging is worked in three sections of color and stitch size.
Section 1: from lower edge base line.
Over eight threads. Color nos. **3., 7., 8., 9., 2., 10., 3.**
Section 2: over six threads. Color nos. **4., 5., 1., 3., 2., 3., 1., 5.**
Section 3: over four threads. Color nos. **1., 12., 11., 6., 10., 5., 1.**
Fill in the part rows at the top and bottom by repeating the color sequence. Block and finish as shown on page 62.
Make cords and balls for trimming as shown on page 62. Stitch to the bottom of the hanging – following the zigzag lines of the pattern if so desired.

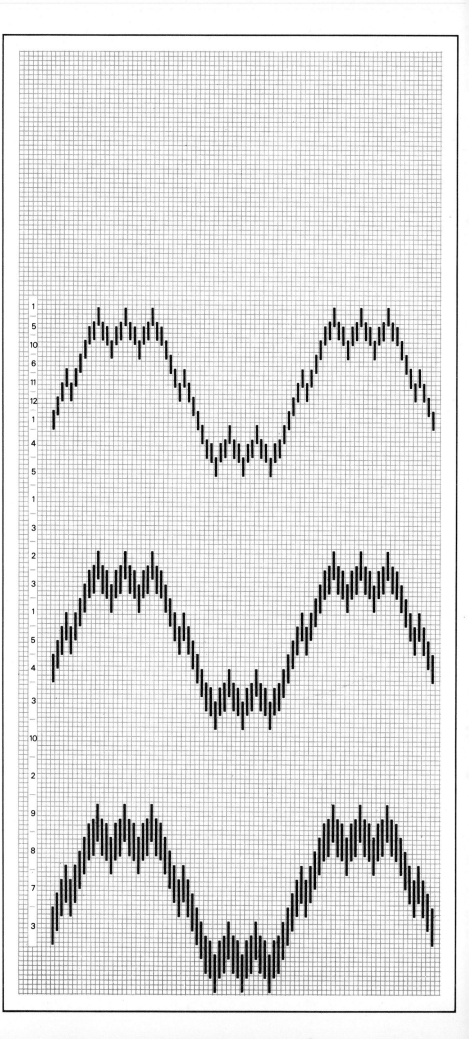

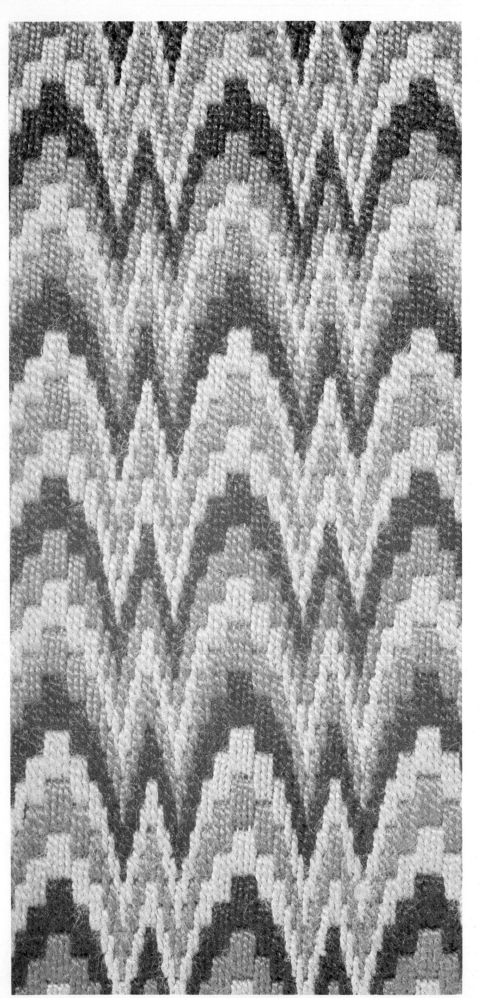

set and match

Florentine upholstered chair and matching drapery tie-back—fit to grace the most elegant of rooms.

Finished measurement: *Chair*, about 16″ wide x 12″ deep. *Tie-back*, about 40″ long x 4″ at widest point.

Fabrics: *Chair*. Single canvas, 16 threads to the inch. See page 13 for instructions for measuring a chair to assess quantity of canvas.

Tie-back. Single canvas, 16 threads to the inch, about 44″ x 10″. For each tie-back, lining 42″ x 8″ and matching button.

Yarn: Pearl Cotton for Linen or a knitting or crochet cotton. **1.** Dark; **2.** Medium; **3.** Light.

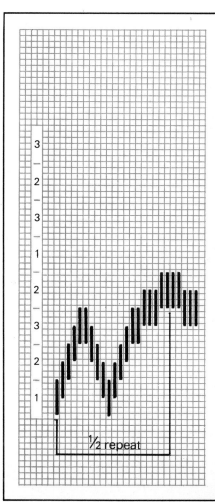

To assess yarn quantity:
About 12 yards of the yarn (used double) is needed to stitch one pattern row across the 16″ width. Count the number of rows in each color and multiply by 12 to assess number of yards required.
Needle: Tapestry, No. 18.
Stitch: Florentine.

Tie-back. Enlarge the given tracing pattern and draw it onto the canvas.
Chair seat. From the instructions on page 13, draw the measured shape onto the canvas. The embroidery is the same for both tie-back and chair. Two lengths of the yarn threaded in the needle should fill the canvas. Work a test piece to find the exact thickness required to fill the canvas. (See page 10 for both how to estimate yarn quantities and how to relate the size of yarn to canvas.) Work in Florentine stitch over six threads and back three. With tone **1.** follow the chart and work a complete row across the center of the canvas up to the traced shape.

Follow with complete rows of the following tones. **2.3.2.1.3.2.3.** These eight rows complete the pattern and are repeated throughout. Continue until the drawn shape on the canvas is covered. Some part rows and half stitches will be needed to fit the drawn outline. Work over the line rather than inside it. The broken edge will be hidden in the finishing. Block and finish as shown on page 62.

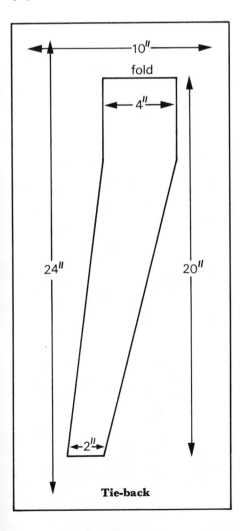

Tie-back

brighten up a chair

Bring an old piece of furniture to life. Work the upholstery in eye-catching Florentine to blend with your decor.

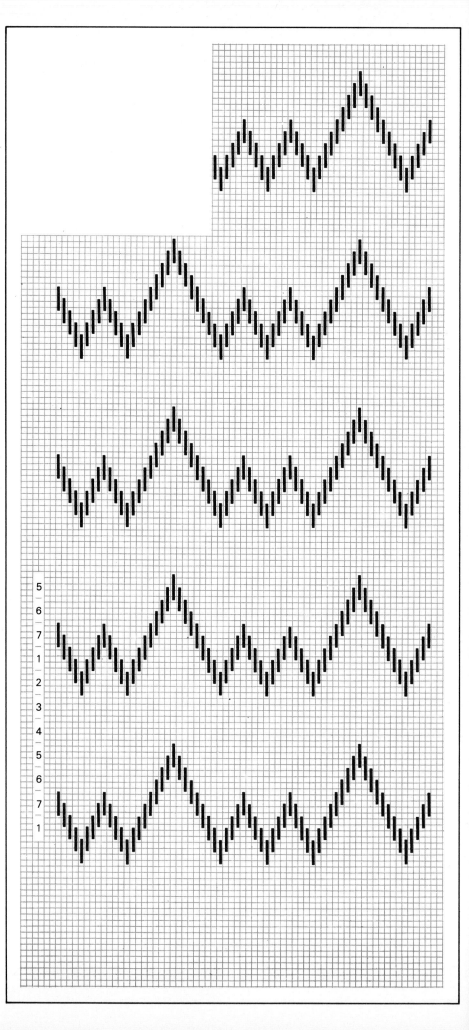

Finished measurement: Top of chair, about 15″ x 13″.

Fabric: Single canvas, 10 threads to the inch. For measuring canvas required, see page 13. 21″ x 19″ is required for the chair shown.

Yarn: D.M.C. Tapestry Wool (used double). Quantities given are for an area 17″ x 15″ which includes 2″ side drops. 4 skeins of each of the following colors.
1. 7407; **2.** 7402; **3.** 7772; **4.** 7769; **5.** 7342; **6.** 7344; **7.** 7384.

Needle: Tapestry, No. 18.

Stitch: Florentine, Method 1. (See page 12).

A suggested back and side drop of about 2 inches is included. Extend the front to the required depth, with a cut-out (which is left plain) as shown for the back of the chair. Mark the centers of the canvas and outline the area of the chair seat. With yarn double in the needle, begin at the top center with color **2.** and work outward. From this complete row, follow on in color sequence until the required area is worked. Fill in the part rows. Block and finish as shown on page 62.

color at your feet

More ideas for Bargello for the home. Dress up a wastepaper basket, or bring a wealth of pattern and color to the hearth.

Fender stool
Finished measurement: About 34″ x 14″. Side drop about 3″.
Fabric: Single canvas, 14 threads to the inch, 38″ x 18″ for the top. For the side drop, 38″ x 17″.
Yarn: Peri-Lusta 3-ply Persian in the following colors. Eight 8.8 yard skeins of each color.
Yellow range: **1.** 446; **2.** 445; **3.** 444; **4.** 443; **5.** 442; Orange range: **6.** 804; **7.** 803; **8.** 802; **9.** 801; Red/coral range: **10.** 706; **11.** 707; **12.** 708; **13.** 709.

Needle: Tapestry, No. 18.
Stitch: Florentine and satin stitch blocks.

The top of the fender stool is worked in Aurora Borealis. (See Pattern Library, page 22.) The side drop is one half of the curvature pattern shown on page 6. Work the Aurora Borealis pattern across the length of the canvas. Work the color sequence as in the listed colors: through yellow, orange and red/coral, then back to yellow. Work each side drop separately, spacing them on the canvas with 2 inches all around each section to allow for finishing. Finish as shown on page 63.

Dress up a waste-paper basket
Finished measurement: Circumference, about 22″. Height about 10″.
Fabric: Single canvas, 14 threads to the inch, 28″ x 14″. Braid; about 24″.
Yarn: Peri-Lusta 3-ply Persian in the following colors. Number of 8.8 yard skeins given in brackets after the color details. **1.** 736 blue (3); **2.** 713 bright green (3); **3.** 256 clover (3); **4.** 258 clover (5); **5.** 257 clover (4); **6.** 223 red (5).
Needle: Tapestry, No. 18.
Stitch: Florentine.

Mark the vertical center of the canvas. Two inches in from one edge, begin the high point of the trellis pattern on this center line. Work the trellis across the canvas to within two inches on all sides. Fill in the color sequence as shown on the chart. This pattern is an adaptation of that shown in the Pattern Library on page 26. Block and finish as shown on page 63.

Hearts are gay
Finished measurement: About 16″ x 13″.
Fabric: Single canvas, 14 threads to the inch, 20″ x 17″.
Yarn: Peri-Lusta 3-ply Persian in the following colors. The number of 8.8 yard skeins is given in brackets after the color number. **1.** 818 (11) dark green; **2.** 713 (11) mid green; **3.** 714 (11) pale green; **4.** 455 (1) white; **5.** 705 (1) bright yellow; **6.** 295 (11) pale yellow.
Needle: Tapestry, No. 18.
Stitch: Florentine.

Mark the horizontal and vertical centers of the canvas. Mark the positions of the five hearts with the center heart on the center lines. The apex of the zigzag design is on the center line. The flame zigzag continues through each heart but with a color change. The majority of the stitching is over 4 threads and back 2. Where the hearts interrupt the background colors, half stitches are worked so that the design stands out clearly. With the flame pattern shown on page 5 as an inspiration, work a similar scheme across the canvas beginning at the center point. For the high point, work about 9 stitches before changing the angle. Continue down the canvas with groups of stitches working all the time over 4 threads and back 2. Stitch the other side of the apex to correspond. Block and finish as shown on page 63.

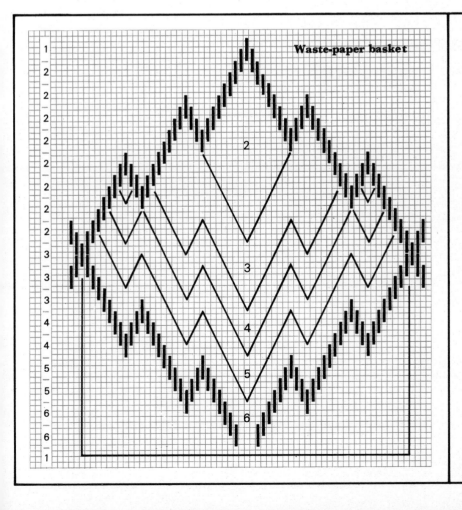

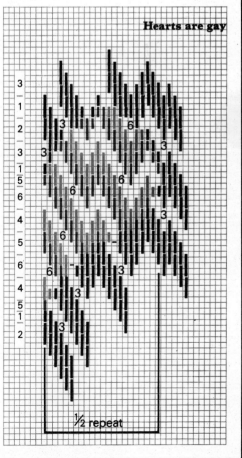

colorful comfort

Easy to make, easy to wear—magnificent carpet slippers and elegant leisure hours for men or women.

Finished measurement: Front depth about 5″, instep about 8½″.

Fabric: Single canvas, 14 threads to the inch, about 14″ x 28″. Lining – ½ yard of 36″. 2 pairs of cork soles.

Yarn: Peri-Lusta 3-ply Persian in the following colors.

Heart – **1.** 360; **2.** 361; **3.** 362. (One 8.8 yard skein of each of this blue range.)

Two zigzags – **4.** 166; **5.** 105; **6.** 145; **7.** 712; **8.** 146; **9.** 711; **10.** 375; **11.** 441. (Two 8.8 skeins of each of this yellow/green range.)

Background stripe – **12.** 362; **13.** 411. (Five 8.8 yard skeins of each of this blue/brown range).

Needle: Tapestry, No. 18.

Stitch: Florentine, satin stitch blocks.

Work the two uppers side by side on the same canvas. Leave at least a 3 inch gap between each for blocking and finishing. Mark the center of the canvas and the vertical and horizontal centers for each of the uppers. Mark two inches in from the edge on the vertical centers and count 32 threads up. Outline the heart from this point. Next work the flame pattern from the toe to the outer instep. The smaller patterns and background stripes are filled in around these basic lines. Block and finish as shown on page 63.

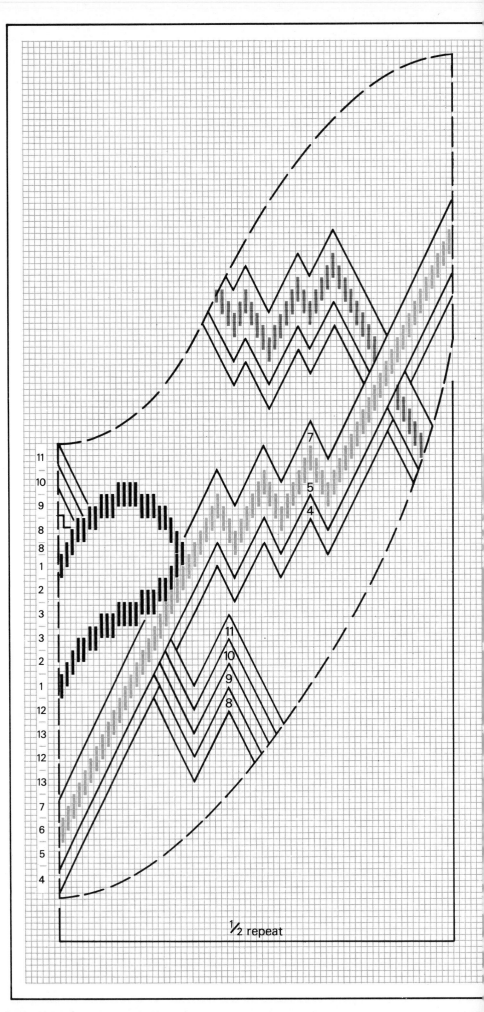

shoulder stroller

Finished measurement: About 11¾″ x 10″. Gusset 1¾″ deep.
Fabric: Two pieces of single canvas, 18 threads to the inch, 16″ x 14″. For the gusset, a strip 37″ x 6″. Lining, ½ yard navy blue poplin.
Yarn: D.M.C. Tapestry Wool. Number of skeins in brackets.

Green range: **1.** 7956 (4); **2.** 7909 (3).
Blue/green range: **3.** 7314 (4); **4.** 7317 (4); **5.** 7820 (4); **6.** 7389 (4); **7.** 7299 (6).
Shoulder strap – 1 skein of each color has been included in the above yarn quantities.
Needle: Tapestry, No. 20.

Work the two sides and the gusset separately. Baste center lines and an area 11¾″ x 10½″. Work from the chart across the 11¾″ width. Follow the color sequence above and below the foundation row. Continue until the area is filled. Work half stitches to complete a straight line at the ends.
Work the opposite side in the same way. The gusset strip is worked across in rows as shown in Brick Stitch. See diagram *right* and instructions for Brick Stitch on page 12. Block and finish as shown on page 63.

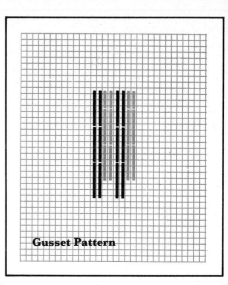

Gusset Pattern

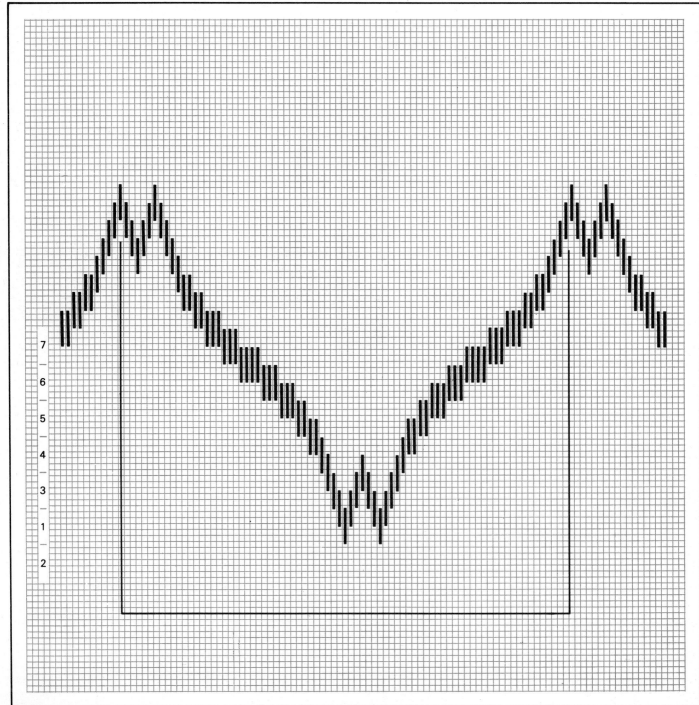

speedy stitchery

Two simply worked, bang up-to-date designs.

Pendant motif sampler bag
Finished measurement: 11″ x 14″.
Fabric: Two pieces of sage green burlap, 15″ x 18″. ½ yard cotton lining.
Yarn: D.M.C. Tapestry Wool, 1 skein of each color. Orange/red range: 7436; 7437; 7947; 7946; 7666. Yellow/brown: 7746; 7745; 7484; 7485; 7477; 7467; 7469. Lime: 7548.
Needle: Tapestry, No. 20.

With basting thread, mark the centers in each direction, keeping to the straight thread of the fabric. Outline an oblong 11″ x 14″. From one end, mark 6 inches along the 14

inch center line. With lime green (7548), outline Pattern 1. Omit stitch block 13 and continue down. Fill in the shape with the subsequent colors in the orange/red range, working from dark to light.
Starting from stitch block 13 and with the tones reversed, work another pattern at each side. From block 1 and with the yellow/brown color range, work Pattern 2. Begin with dark brown (7467). Outline the inner Pattern 5A and 7A, from block 6 upward. Finish with rows of Brick stitch as shown. Block and finish as on page 63.

Key to the pendant design

1. and **3.** Orange/red range. 7436; 7437; 7947; 7946; 7666; 7544; lime green.
2. Reverse colors for 1 and 3. Omit 7436. Finish center with 7746.
4. and **6.** 7666; skip four threads; 7946; 7947; 7436.
5. Work as **7.** Reverse order of shading in 5A from that in 7A.
7. Brown/yellow range. 7469; 7467; 7477; 7485; 7484; 7745; 7746. **7A.** 7469; 7467; 7485; 7484; 7745.

Zigzag design sampler bag
Finished measurement: 11″ x 14″.
Fabric: Two pieces of sage green burlap, 15″ x 18″. ½ yard cotton for lining.
Yarn: D.M.C. Tapestry Wool, 1 skein of each color. Yellow/brown range. 7446; 7745; 7484; 7485; 7477; 7467; 7469.
Needle: Tapestry, No. 20.

This incorporates a simple zigzag pattern in one color range. It shows the related angles of the same design. The outer edge is worked over four and back two threads, half its length. The center follows the same design lines and is worked over six threads and back two, one third its length.
The highest point at each side crosses over and interlocks at the center.
Mark the centers and 11″ x 14″ area with basting thread. Begin with dark brown yarn 7469; and work over four and back two threads as on the foundation row of the chart. Continue through the color range and repeat at the opposite side. Change to working over six and back two threads and repeat the stitch and color order. Finish as shown on page 63.

Pendant Motif 1

Pendant Motif 2

Zigzag Design

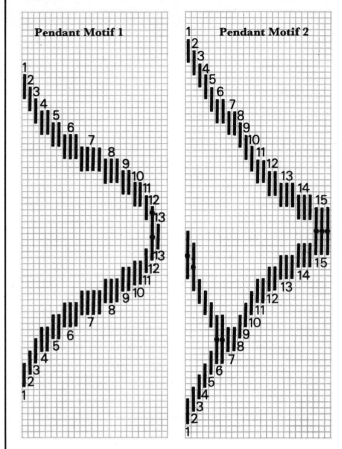

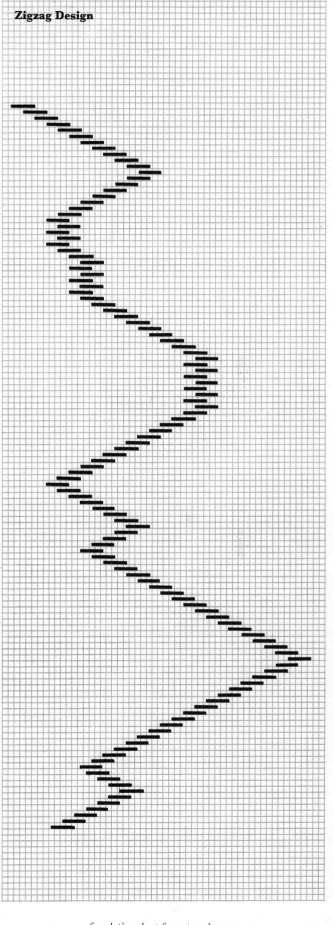

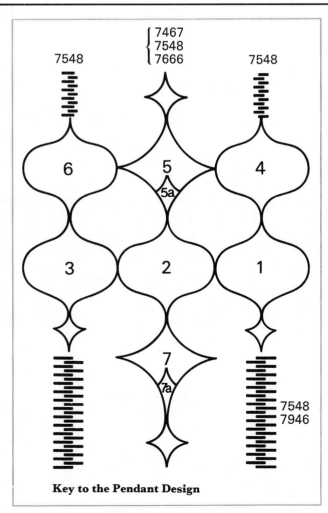

Key to the Pendant Design

foundation chart for outer edge row

coats of many colors

Op-art pattern, vibrant color scheme and luxurious trimming all combine in this eye-catching winter jacket. In complete contrast left Florentine also lends itself to somewhat softer visual appeal. Instructions on how to adapt your Florentine work to garments with shaping are on page 55.

shaping up with florentine

A knock-out Florentine vest, worked back and front in rich assortments of pattern and color.

Choose a commercial pattern, with as simple a shape as possible. See page 13 for instructions on how to draw the pattern onto canvas. The pattern in the vest shown was built up by first stitching the belt in the waist position, and then working upward and downward from this section. It is possible to combine many of the different patterns illustrated in this book to work such a garment. It also presents an opportunity for using up small quantities of yarn left over from other designs. Instructions for turnings, darts and linings can be found on page 60. This vest has been worked in a wide range of Peri-Lusta shades.

Left Silk jersey dress, attractively bib-fronted with bold Florentine.

Below Embroidered hat worn with matching top over sweater and gauchos.

Embroidered Florentine blazer, worked on canvas, with matching cloche hat.

fashion ideas for florentine

Florentine embroidered vest, with large patch pockets bound in suede.

Embroidered vest (evenweave linen) and matching scarf, over jersey jump suit.

Florentine embroidered top with matching natty shorts and belt.

Curly sheepskin jacket
with collar, cuffs and
pockets all in Florentine.

Crewel wool Florentine jerkin
over silk shirt and Oxford
bags. Hat to tone.

Lightweight woolen smock
with embroidered yoke
over dress in sheer fabric.

*Smock inserts on sleeves
and front, all embroidered
in colorful Florentine.*

*Tucked smock with Florentine
belt tying with plaited,
woolen thongs. Matching shorts.*

*Florentine embroidered
smock with front opening, over
silk blouse and jersey pants.*

finishing instructions

Blocking finished needlepoint
You will need a flat board, new blotting paper and drawing pins. Lay two or three thicknesses of blotting paper on the board and dampen thoroughly. With the embroidery face upward on the blotting paper, pin from the center of the top edge and work outward. Align the canvas with the straight edge of the board. Repeat at the opposite end and for the two sides. Leave to dry for at least twenty-four hours.

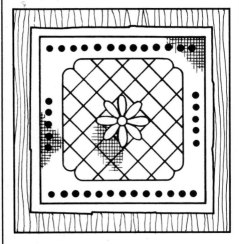

Finishing
Good finishing is vital to the splendor of the finished embroidery. In making up Florentine embroidery, the aim is to cover the canvas threads just as in the stitching. This is achieved by taking the seam stitching just into the embroidery.
The angular quality of the needlepoint is emphasized by good shaping. The squares of the canvas are useful guide lines toward easy making up. Avoid cutting the seam allowance until basting, fitting and stitching are correct. If alterations have to be made, there is sufficient canvas to add one or two more stitches of embroidery – or to readjust a shaping without fear of the canvas fraying. Cotton poplin, fine denim or similar closely woven fabrics are all firm linings to support the comparatively heavy embroidery.

Turnings, darts and linings
Choose a simple commercial pattern so that shaping is minimal. Before beginning the embroidery, mark the outline (excluding seam allowance), darts and shapings onto the canvas; but do not cut out. Carry the embroidery up to the marked shapings. When the embroidery is complete, back stitch the darts by hand, making sure that the stitching is taken just into the embroidery. When a dart has to be clipped and pressed open, stitch seam binding over the cut edges to prevent fraying. Stitch flat with a loose herringbone stitch. Baste seams, and machine or hand stitch, again taking the

stitching just into the embroidery. Cut seam allowance and immediately make the edges neat with seam binding.
Finish and insert the lining as instructed in the bought pattern.

Hairband
Cut off the spare canvas five threads from the edge of the embroidery. Trim the lining material to the same size. Turn excess canvas to the back of the work, mitering the corners. Make turnings on the lining and attach the lining to the canvas, wrong sides facing. Slip stitch along the long edges. Cut a length of the elastic and slot the ends into the open ends of the hairband, between canvas and lining. Stitch firmly into place. Slip stitch to close ends.

Compact case
After blocking work as shown on this page, trim excess canvas to within 5 threads of the embroidery, line the work and slip stitch all around. Fold the work in half across the width, pin and whip stitch the edges together. Leave ¼ inch open at the lower corners to tuck in the ends of cord. Slip stitch the cord up one side, across the top and down the other side. Secure the cord firmly at the corners.

Glasses case
Block the work as shown on this page and trim the canvas. Cut the lining to the same size. Attach the lining to the needlepoint, with wrong sides together, and slip stitch closed. Fold the work across the width, 5½ inches from the end, and slip stitch the two side seams, leaving ¼ inch open at the corners. Tuck the cord ends into the corners and stitch in place. Cut a piece of cord 3½ inches long, to secure the flap. Tuck the ends of the cord into the side seams at the mouth of the pocket and stitch in place. The flap tucks under this cord to keep the case closed.

Lighter case
Block the canvas as shown on this page and trim off the excess. Cut the lining to the same size as the canvas work and attach the lining as instructed for the hairband. Fold the work in half and stitch the side seams, leaving ¼ inch open at the corners for inserting the ends of cord. Insert the ends of the cord into the corners and stitch the cord neatly into place on three sides of the case, leaving one of the opening edges without cord trim. If you wish, make handmade cords using one or more of the various yarns used in the embroidery.

Cushions
Feathers, plastic foam or kapok are all suitable fillings for pillow forms. Make the forms of the same shape but slightly smaller than the cover. Use sufficient filling. A pillow is most comfortable if it is firm without being too hard.

Pin and baste right sides together. Stitch, leaving one end open to insert the pillow form.
Trim seam and turn to the right side. Insert form, turn in seam allowance and close the opening with slip stitches.

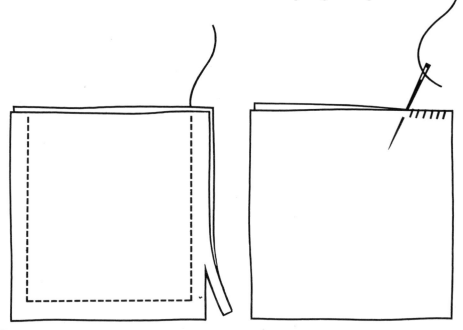

Belts

Interline and line as shown for the tie-back on page 62.

Belt with bought buckle.

Mitered end. Trim the canvas as shown, before interlining and lining.

Square end. Fold in the lining and the canvas, and overcast together. Thread around the center bar of the buckle and stitch in place.

Belts with embroidered square buckle and medallion buckle.

Trim around the medallions very carefully. Snip into the corners and immediately overcast to prevent the canvas fraying. Line and interline, once again as for the tie-back. Close the belt with large snap fasteners.

Clasp belt.

Line this belt as for the hairband, leave the buckle end flat and overcast the raw edges together. Place the buckle over the end of the belt, fold over 1½ inches, and stitch firmly in place.

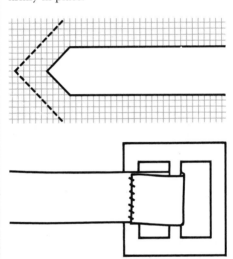

Caftan trim

Clip the seam allowance of the embroidery to one inch. Turn in and herringbone to the back of the embroidery. For the neck opening, overcast the two diagonal strips together for the required number of stitches to form the mitered trim. Pin the finished pieces in position on the caftan and stitch in place. Bring the needle up from the caftan and down into the applied pieces, taking a longer stitch at the back and a straight stitch at the front.

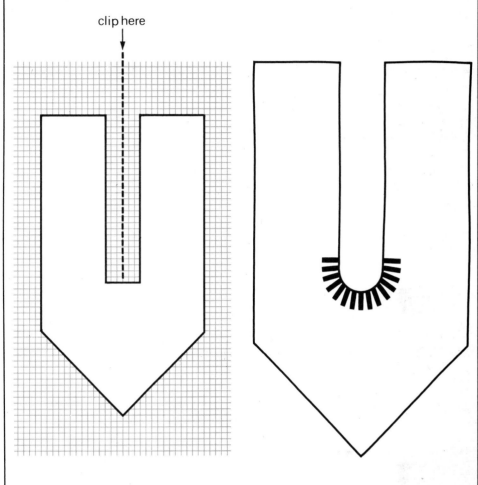

Flap-over bag with gusset

Cut the lining and interlining for both the gusset and bag. Baste the interlining in position on the bag. Cut the surplus canvas to within half an inch of the embroidery. Fold the seam allowance over the interlining and herringbone stitch in position. Cut the lining and baste just within the back-stitched line. Slip stitch the lining to the bag. Cut and make the gussets in the same way. Press a center fold so that the bag closes neatly. Fold the length of embroidery into three, matching the flap to the front patterns. Begin from the center point and pin, baste and overcast the gussets into position. Finish with a snap fastener at the center of the flap.

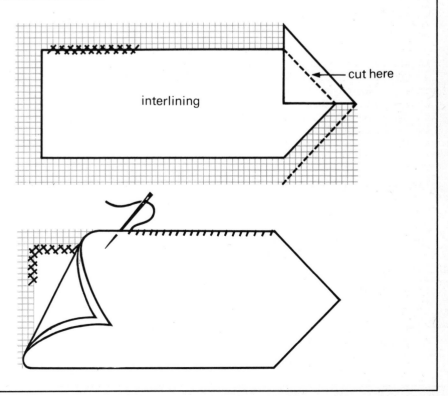

Rugs and Wallhangings

Rugs may be either lined or left unlined. If lined, there is a tendency for grit to cut the threads between the back of the embroidery and the lining. Unlined, these will fall straight through. Natural burlap, or an equally firm but loosely woven fabric makes a good lining. The method for making and lining all flat objects is the same. For an unlined rug, turn in and herringbone to the back as shown. Make the hem neat with carpet webbing stitched over the turnings. For extra strength in large carpets and wall hangings, leave the seam allowance intact. Where there is to be a lining, leave one inch turning on a heavy weight fabric. For medium weight, $\frac{1}{2}$-$\frac{3}{4}$ inch will be sufficient. Slip stitch the lining in position as shown on page 61 for the handbag. For a large hanging or rug, more than 36″ in either direction, lock the lining to the canvas. That is, take loose slip stitches into the embroidery and the wrong side of the lining at the center and at about two foot intervals. The wall hanging shown on page 39 is unlined, but the weight of the embroidery insures that it hangs well. To fit the batten, turn the wide hem at the top to form a sleeve and slip the batten into the center. Some adjustment may be necessary so that the hanging is level.

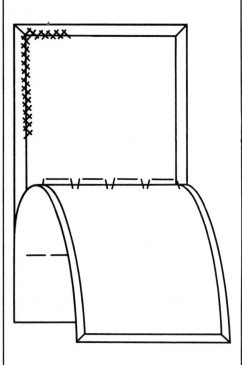

A drop-in chair seat

Match the embroidery to the vertical and horizontal centers of the upholstery. Pin in place. Smooth and block evenly as you pin so that the embroidery stitches lie in straight lines. Using chair tacks, fasten the canvas to the back of the seat. Check as you work to make sure that the embroidery is taut. Continue nailing, working outward from the centers.

Wool ball trimming

Cut two circles from thin cardboard. Cut a hole at the center. The diameter of the tassel will be at least that of the circle of cardboard. Place the two cardboard circles together and oversew closely with long lengths of yarn. Fill the cardboard. Insert scissors between the two cardboard circles and clip the yarn. Fasten a thread securely between the cardboards, which are then cut to the center hole and removed.

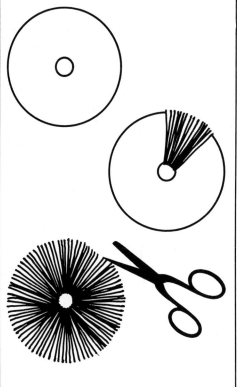

Tie-back for draperies

An interlining is an optional stiffening. Cut the interlining slightly within the size of the embroidered area, and a lining with a seam allowance of half an inch. Baste the interlining to the wrong side of the embroidery. Cut the blocking allowance of the canvas to $\frac{1}{2}$ inch for a fine canvas and up to 1 inch for a coarse one. Turn and herringbone to the interlining and line as in the 'Handbag with gusset' instructions on page 61.

The tie-backs fasten with a button and loop. Before closing the lining at each end, stitch the button in position and make a buttonhole loop with matching yarn at the opposite end. Use two or three strands so that the loop is in proportion to the embroidery and of a size which will slip easily over the button. Work in close buttonhole over the yarn loop.

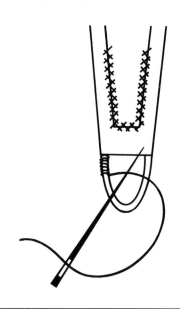

Mitered corners for a chair seat or stool

The canvas is marked as shown, and the embroidery taken up to the four corner cutouts. When finishing, fold into a box shape, open out and fold diagonally at the corners. With the wrong side facing, backstitch the embroidered edges together. Fold in the corner shapings and slip stitch into position.

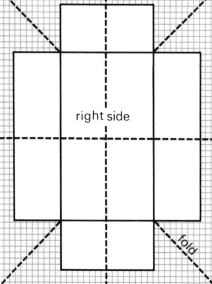

right side

fold

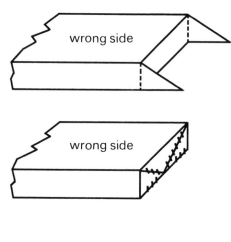

wrong side

wrong side

Waste paper basket

Seam together the two ends of the rectangle. Press seam open. Slide the joined canvas over the bin from the bottom upward, and decorate the top with braid. Cut a length of braid to fit the top of the bin, allowing $\frac{1}{2}$ inch for turnings. Fix in place with small dabs of fabric glue.

Footstool with hearts

Trim the canvas to $1\frac{1}{2}$ inches, and turn the seam allowance to the wrong side. Herringbone stitch in position. Pin the canvas to the upholstered top of the stool so that it is correctly centered. Fix a brass headed tack at the center of each side. Work outward, fixing the tacks closely and adjusting the canvas to fit the edge of the stool.

Fender stool

Cut out the four strips for the side drops. Leave one inch on all sides. With right sides together, join the four narrow ends with a back stitch. Use a strong thread such as buttonhole twist. Stitch close to the embroidery – just into rather than outside it – so that the canvas threads are completely covered. As each join is made, check for fit at the corners of the stool. With right sides together, back stitch the top to the sides. Turn the lower edge to the wrong side and herringbone stitch in positions. Fit the cover to the stool and secure with brass-headed tacks.

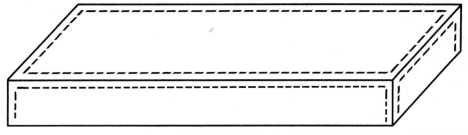

Slippers

Interline and line the slipper tops as shown for the tie-back on page 62. Using the insoles as a pattern, cut two right and two left foot pieces from the lining fabric. Allow $\frac{1}{2}$ inch turning. Run a gathering thread around the outer edge of the lining. Draw up to fit the sole; and with fabric glue, stick into position. Lightly pin the embroidered upper in position. This is easiest with the pins in the edge of the sole. Fold and stick turnings in position. Stick the second sole in position. Overcast the edges for extra security.

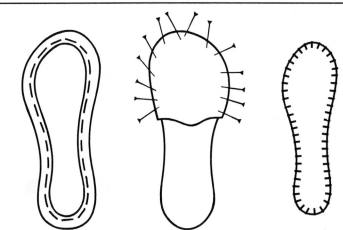

Shoulder stroller

With right sides together, baste and machine stitch the gusset to the two sides. Cut out and make the lining in the same manner.

Trim the lining and canvas, leaving a 1 inch turning at the top. With wrong sides together, insert the lining into the bag. Turn in and slip stitch at the top.

Make a series of cords using a skein of each color. Follow the instructions for cord making given below, and adjust the size as desired. Finish the top opening of the bag with navy blue cord; and with the remaining six cords, braid into a color sequence as in the embroidery. Stitch firmly in position at the sides of the bag, concealing the stitching with a piece of the navy cord.

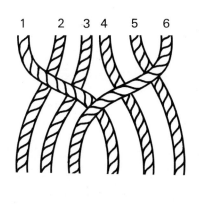

How to make a cord

Measure two and a half times the required length for the cord. Four or five lengths will make a cord of suitable size for a piping around needlepoint. At least ten to twelve lengths will be needed for a bag handle. Tie the lengths together at each end. Fasten one end to a fixed point, the other to a pencil. Turn the pencil clockwise until the ends are well twisted together. Fold in half, fasten the two ends again and turn anti-clockwise. Pull sharply to lock the cord. Knot the ends, leaving a fringe for decoration.

This cord is suitable for use with the Shoulder Stroller shown on page 48.

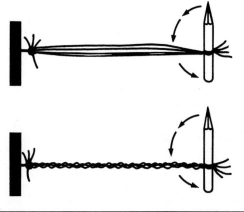

Sampler bags

Press the embroidery on the wrong side into a well padded ironing board. Baste and machine stitch the two sides with right sides together, leaving the top open. Cut and stitch a lining in the same manner, making it slightly smaller than the bag so that it lies smoothly. Trim seams of bag and lining, leaving $\frac{3}{4}$ inch turning at the top. Fit the lining into the bag, turn in the two upper edges and slip stitch together. Make a cord as shown above, using the remaining lengths of yarn. Stitch to the sides of the bag. concealing the stitches in the twist of the cord.

Subtle yet splendid: cream and chocolate variations with both traditional and contemporary decors in mind. The scope for Florentine is indeed never-ending . . . .

64